Easy-to-Make
DOLLS
with Nineteenth-Century
Costumes

by G.P. Jones

Dover Publications, Inc., New York

Published in Canada by General Publishing Company,
Ltd., 30 Lesmill Road, Don Mills, Toronto, Ontario.
Published in the United Kingdom by Constable and
Company, Ltd., 10 Orange Street, London WC2H 7EG.

Easy-to-Make Dolls with Nineteenth-Century Costumes is
a new work, first published by Dover Publications, Inc., in
1977.

International Standard Book Number: 0-486-23426-6
Library of Congress Catalog Card Number: 76-24566

Manufactured in the United States of America
Dover Publications, Inc.
180 Varick Street
New York, N.Y. 10014

Contents

Introduction	1
Doll Body Patterns	5
Underwear Patterns	13
Josephine, 1820's	24
Victoria, 1830's	30
Mistress Black, 1830's	38
Pretty Rags, 1840's	46
Melissa, 1850's	54
Belle, 1860's	60
Jocelyn, 1870's	66
Penelope, 1890's	74
Seminole Lady	80
Hiruko, a Lady of Japan	86

Introduction

The dolls presented in this book are not only fun to make, but also a mini-history of fashion during the nineteenth century. The faces, as well as the clothing and hairdos, reflect the styles of the times, as found in paintings, drawings and periodicals. For example, Josephine's face is fashioned after folk-art paintings of the early 1800's. Anyone fortunate enough to own a copy of *Godey's Lady's Book*, a nineteenth-century magazine for women, will immediately recognize Jocelyn's homely face as almost a trademark from its pages. I have included an American Indian doll and a Japanese doll so that there will be dolls representing different ethnic groups in the collection.

The dress patterns have been simplified as much as possible, so that even a novice seamstress can create the fashion silhouettes of the different periods. Those who enjoy handstitching, embroidery, tatting, and so forth, can make the costumes more elaborate, and even more authentic, by indulging in these arts for trims, underwear and decoration of the costumes. Keep in mind that these are basic patterns and can be made just as elaborate as your imagination will allow.

There are two patterns given for making the doll bodies, but the same basic method is used to sew all of the dolls. Josephine, Victoria, Mistress Black, Pretty Rags, Melissa, Belle, Seminole Lady and Hiruko are all made from the same basic doll pattern, appearing on pages 5-9. Special "lady body" patterns for Jocelyn and Penelope appear on pages 10-11. The patterns for the faces for each doll are located with that individual doll's dress pattern. The dresses for dolls made with the same body are interchangeable. You can, therefore, make one doll and use other dress patterns to sew an extensive wardrobe of nineteenth-century fashions for your doll.

Select the doll that you are going to make, and locate the necessary body, underwear and costume pattern pieces. Trace the appropriate patterns from the book and use them as you would any dressmaking pattern. I do not advise cutting the patterns out of the book because this would render any patterns on the underside unusable.

All clothing pattern pieces have a ¼″ seam allowance (unless otherwise stated). There are *no* seam allowances given on the body pattern pieces. This enables you to trace an accurate seamline on your fabric, adding a ¼″ seam allowance as you cut out the pieces. Mark around each pattern with a pencil on the wrong side of the material, leaving space between the pieces for the seam allowance. Cut ¼″ outside the pencil line. This will give you your seam allowance. Sew the pieces together by matching the pencil lines and sewing along these lines. If the seam allowance is not perfect, this will not show; but the sewing line will be perfectly straight and true.

To transfer the necessary markings on the pattern to the fabric, use dressmaker's carbon or graphite paper. Do *not* use typewriter carbon; it will smudge and rub off on the fabric and is almost impossible to remove. Dressmaker's carbon, available at notions, fabric and dime stores, comes in packs of assorted colors in strips about 7″ × 20″. It has a hard waxy finish and is designed for this purpose. Remember to trace darts on the wrong side of the fabric, and the features and hairline on the right side of the fabric. Try to trace lightly, applying just enough pressure so that you can see the lines without their showing through the fabric.

FABRICS TO USE IN DOLL MAKING

For the doll bodies, choose a tightly woven fabric, such as broadcloth or poplin. Percale is often suggested; however, I find that it is too thin to be stuffed as tightly as a doll should be stuffed to hold its shape. The better the grade of fabric used, the more satisfied you will be with the results. I prefer to use a pale peach color, rather than pink. It looks much more natural. For the ethnic dolls, use a hint of the shade, rather than the color of real skin. For example, Mistress Black is the color of cocoa, rather than black. The Seminole Lady is a very pale rust color. Hiruko is the color of unbleached muslin. *Never* use yellow for an Oriental doll. Oriental skin is not yellow, and the result is hideous.

For clothing, look for fabrics that are drapeable, but at the same time will not ravel easily. Keep in mind that the pattern pieces are small and will ravel with handling. For example, a poor choice would be crepe back satin, as it will ravel before you can get it sewn. You can, however, use regular satin. Cotton lining will do nicely as a substitute for hard-to-find colored batiste. When choosing prints, keep them small, in scale with the doll's size.

For trims, try to use laces that have the look of hand crochet or tatting. Velvet and grosgrain ribbons are always good, as is cotton eyelet.

In my list of materials, I have often not indicated whether fabrics should be 24", 36" or 45" wide because I want you to be uninhibited in your choice of fabrics. If you have a piece left over from other sewing projects or if you find a remnant that you like, feel free to use it. Your finished skirt will be fuller or narrower depending upon the width of the fabric.

If you use washable fabrics, stuff your doll with polyester stuffing and use synthetic yarn for the hair, your doll will be washable.

MATERIALS FOR DOLL MAKING

A list of materials needed to complete each doll accompanies the instructions for making the individual doll. I have not included in my list stuffing for bodies or the general things that you will have available in your sewing box, such as sewing thread. In addition here are some things that you may not have in your sewing box that will be handy for making your dolls:

1. A very long needle—5" upholstery needle is ideal for attaching arms.
2. Colored pencils for shading faces.
3. Powdered rouge for rosy cheeks.
4. White textile paint for eyes of dark-skinned dolls.
5. Cotton cord or ⅛" elastic for attaching arms to body.
6. Woven straw ¼" wide, or old straw hats which can be taken apart and used for your doll hats.

SEWING THE DOLL BODIES

1. Use tiny stitches and polyester thread. Stitch darts in body front and back.
2. Where necessary, stitch seat to body back, matching notches.
3. Right sides together, stitch around sides and head of body. Hold one set of darts in one direction, the other set in opposite direction, to avoid bulk. Leave open across lower edge of body for stuffing. Reinforce neck with second row of stitches, right over the first.
4. Stitch arms, leaving open between dots at top for stuffing.
5. Stitch center front and center back leg seams. The foot is left open for stuffing.
6. Carefully clip curved edges, trim seams of hands, and turn all pieces right side out.
7. Place center front and center back seams of legs together, and run a row of stitching across top of leg, about ½" from the edge. This will allow the doll's legs to hang straight. Making sure that the feet face front, stitch tops of legs to seat on body back. The front of body is still open for stuffing.
8. Begin stuffing body. *You must stuff firmly.* This cannot be stressed enough. Stuff head down to about the nose, then insert neck reinforcement. This can be a popsicle stick, a blunt dowel or stick. Do not use sharp pointed objects or wire. This can be very dangerous if a

child should play with the doll. Continue stuffing to lower edge of body. Slip stitch body opening closed.
9. Stuff legs through feet. If you wish your doll to bend at the knees, stuff to the knee point; stitch across; complete stuffing of leg.
10. Run a hand gathering stitch around sole of foot. Insert plastic sole, and pull up gathers. Slip stitch sole of foot to leg, adding more stuffing, if necessary, to give a good, firm foot.
11. Lightly stuff hand. If you want your doll to have fingers, stitch fingers by hand or machine (hand stitching looks better). Finish stuffing arm *firmly.* Slip stitch top of arm closed.
12. Attach arms with cotton cord or ⅛" wide elastic. Run a long needle (mine is a 5" upholstery needle) through one arm, through body at shoulder points, then through other arm. Tie large knots in cord or elastic, close to body, so that arms are moveable, but not hanging.
13. You are now ready to embroider features and apply hair, according to the individual instructions for the doll you are making. After making countless dolls, I have found that the best results are obtained by embroidering the features *after* stuffing. Embroidering the features first often results in a puckered face.

If you use a knot in your embroidery or leave even a tiny tail, it will show through the fabric. When the embroidery is done on a properly stuffed head after the doll is finished, the tension of the stitches is exactly right and no tails or knots can show through. Hair must be done after stuffing because seams are covered with stitches. This technique of embroidering the hair on makes the styles permanent so that when the doll is played with, the hair style is not disturbed. All stitching should be done just under the "skin" so that there is little or no problem with catching in the stuffing.

SEWING DOLL OF FELT

You will need approximately ¼ yard peach or pale pink felt, 72" wide. Be sure that you use good quality, all-wool felt. The type with rayon in it (usually sold in small pieces) will not tolerate being stuffed as hard as your doll should be stuffed; it pulls apart.

The entire doll is sewn by hand, using ladder stitch (*not* slip stitch). Reinforce stitching at beginning and end of stitching, so that stitching will not pull out. No seam allowance is necessary, and to eliminate bulk, cut out darts.

Assemble doll as explained for the cloth doll. Apply features and hair as explained in individual directions for the doll you are making.

Ladder Stitch For Sewing Felt

USING BODY PATTERNS FOR CHINA HEADS

The body patterns are easily converted to use with china heads and limbs.

For basic body front and back, simply draw a gently curving line between dots at neck edge. For limbs, line up china parts with fingertips and feet on cloth pattern. Draw a straight line across pattern ¼" above groove in china part. This is the cutoff point for the cloth portion of arms and legs, and will keep your doll's figure in proportion.

Stitch around three sides of body, leaving open at bottom to stuff. Sew center front and center back seams on limbs, leaving open at top and bottom. With limb pieces still inside out, insert china parts, making sure that they face the center front of cloth pieces. (China parts will be inside cloth pieces). Now, cover the china part with glue at the groove. Tie tightly with string or cord in the groove of china part. Turn right side out and stuff.

To use lady body pattern, follow directions above, except leave the top of body piece open, as well as bottom. When you are ready to attach the china head, this will be gathered closed, to give a fuller bustline.

To attach head to either body, thread a piece of narrow twill tape or strong ribbon through the holes in china head and slip stitch securely to body.

METRIC CONVERSIONS

⅛" — 3mm	6" — 15cm
¼" — 6mm	8" — 20cm
⅜" — 10mm	9" (¼ yard) — 23cm
½" — 13mm	12" (⅓ yard) — 30cm
⅝" — 15mm	18" (½ yard) — 46cm
¾" — 19mm	24" — 62cm
1" — 25mm	27" (¾ yard) — 69cm
1½" — 38mm	36" (1 yard) — 92cm
2" — 50mm	45" (1¼ yards) — 114cm
3" — 76mm	54" (1½ yards) — 137cm
4" — 10cm	72" (2 yards) — 183cm

Doll Body
Patterns

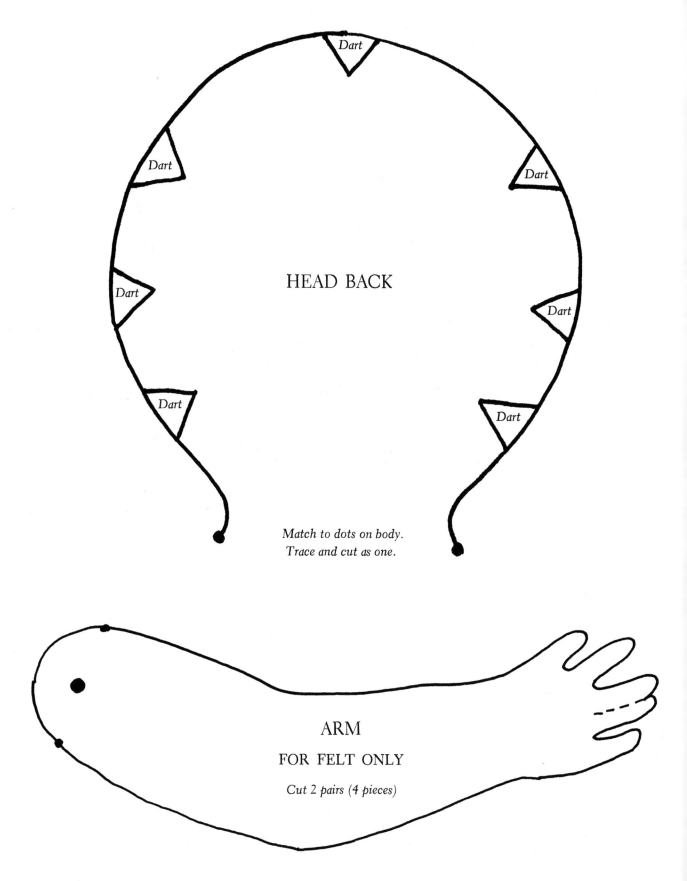

HEAD BACK

Match to dots on body.
Trace and cut as one.

ARM

FOR FELT ONLY

Cut 2 pairs (4 pieces)

ALLOW FOR ALL SEAMS WHEN CUTTING

Match to dots on head.
Trace and cut as one.
BASIC BODY FRONT

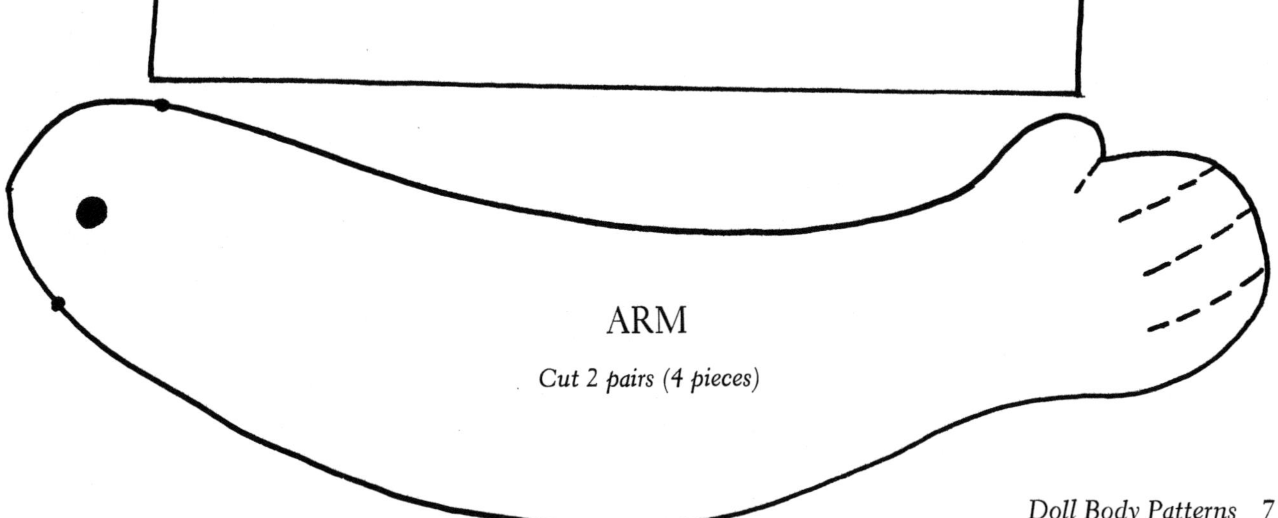

ARM
Cut 2 pairs (4 pieces)

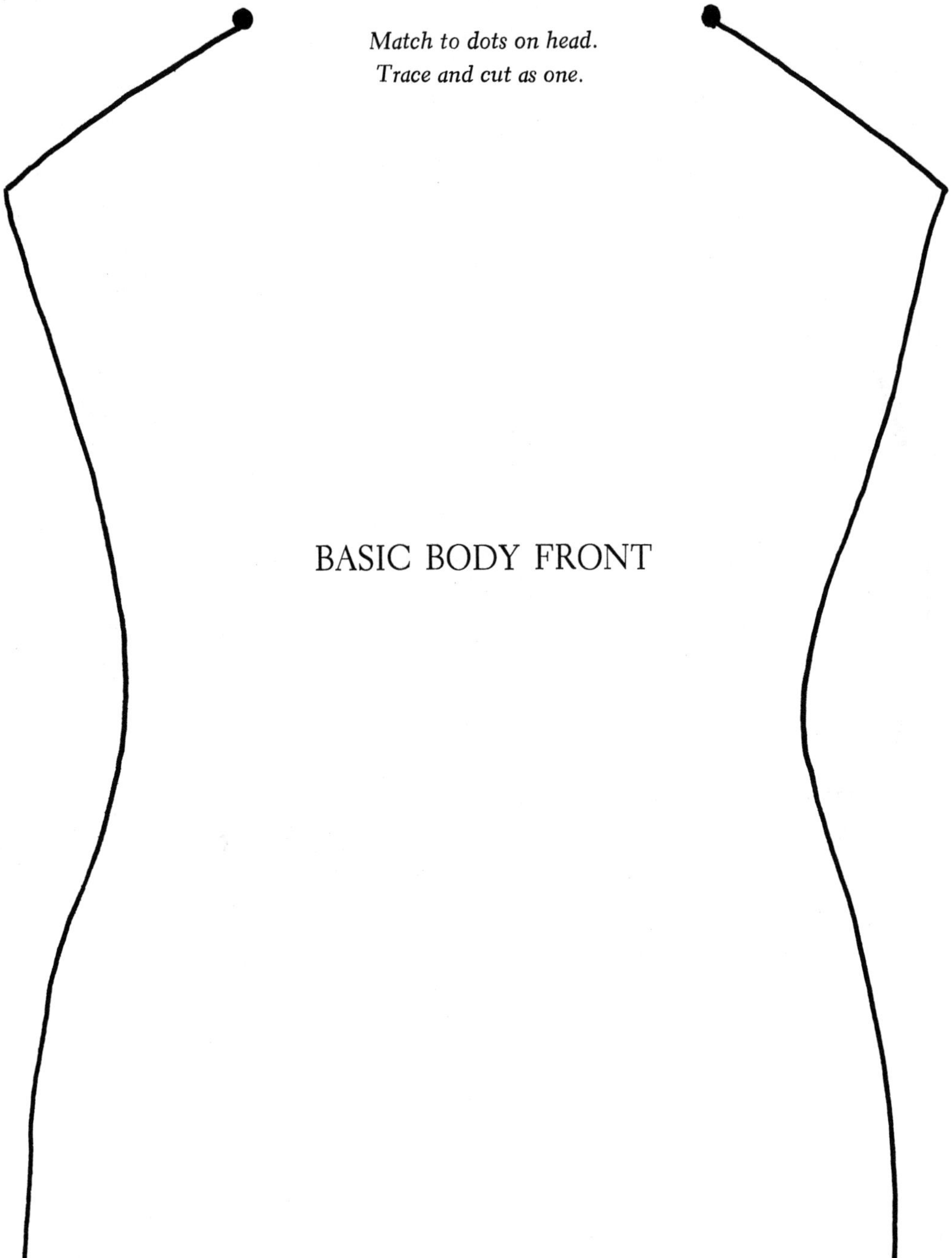

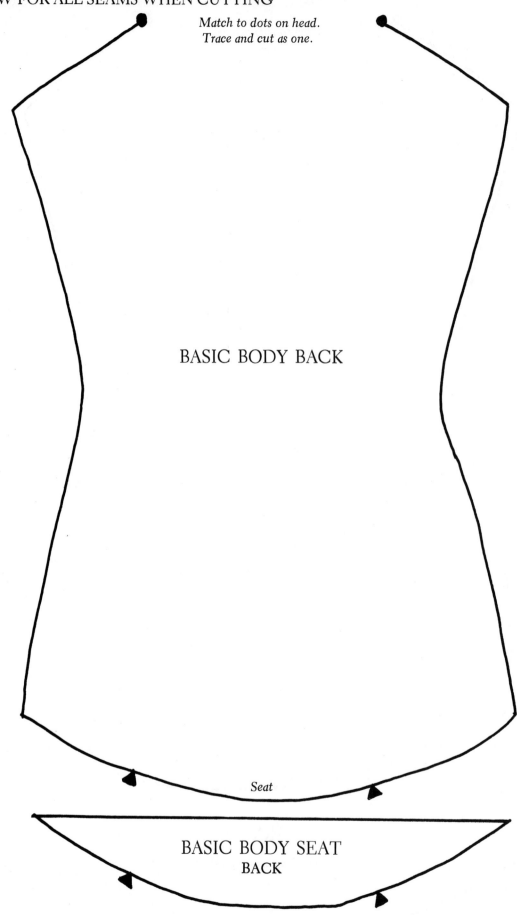

Match to dots on head.
Trace and cut as one.

BASIC BODY BACK

Seat

BASIC BODY SEAT
BACK

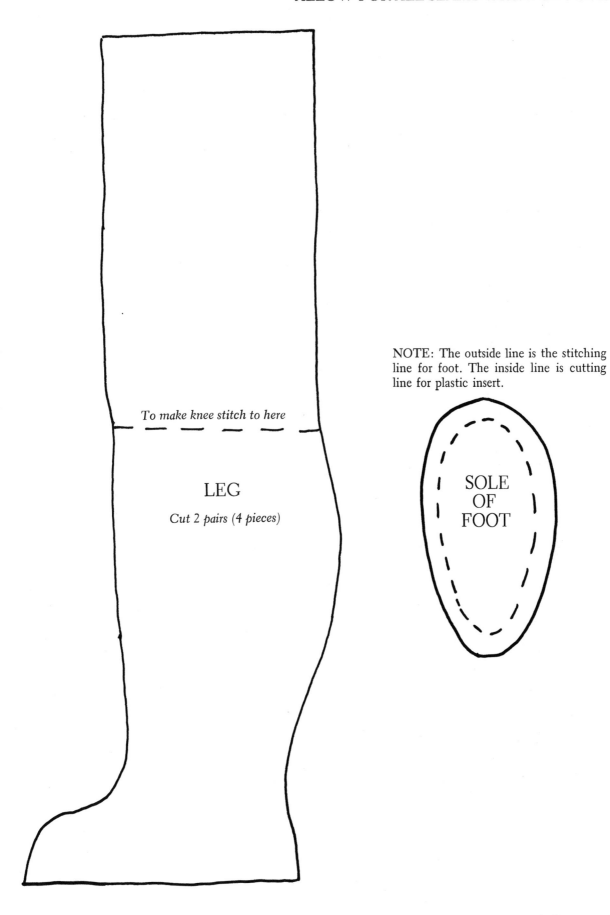

NOTE: The outside line is the stitching line for foot. The inside line is cutting line for plastic insert.

To make knee stitch to here

LEG

Cut 2 pairs (4 pieces)

SOLE
OF
FOOT

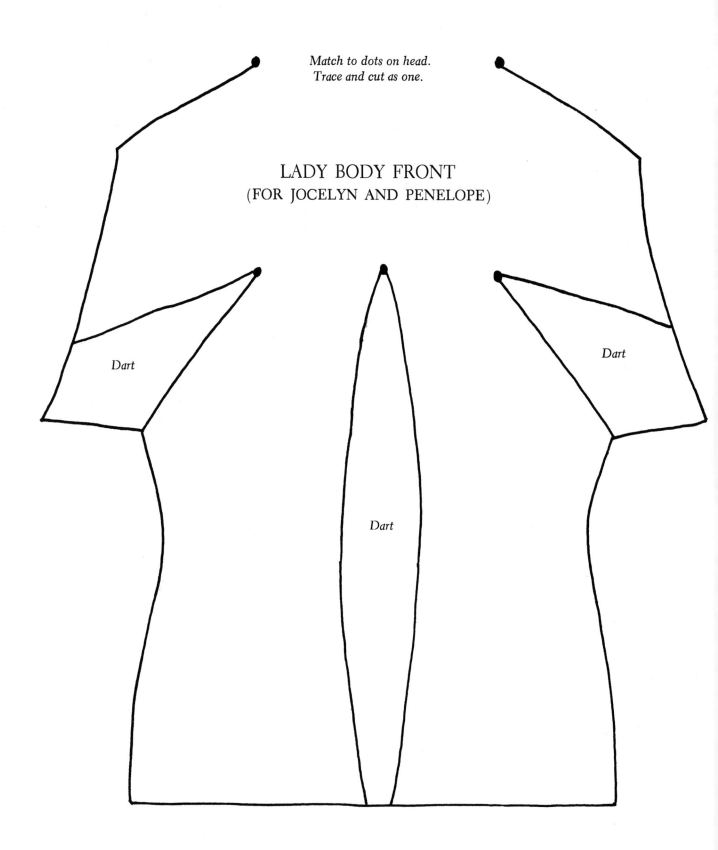

Match to dots on head.
Trace and cut as one.

LADY BODY FRONT
(FOR JOCELYN AND PENELOPE)

Dart

Dart

Dart

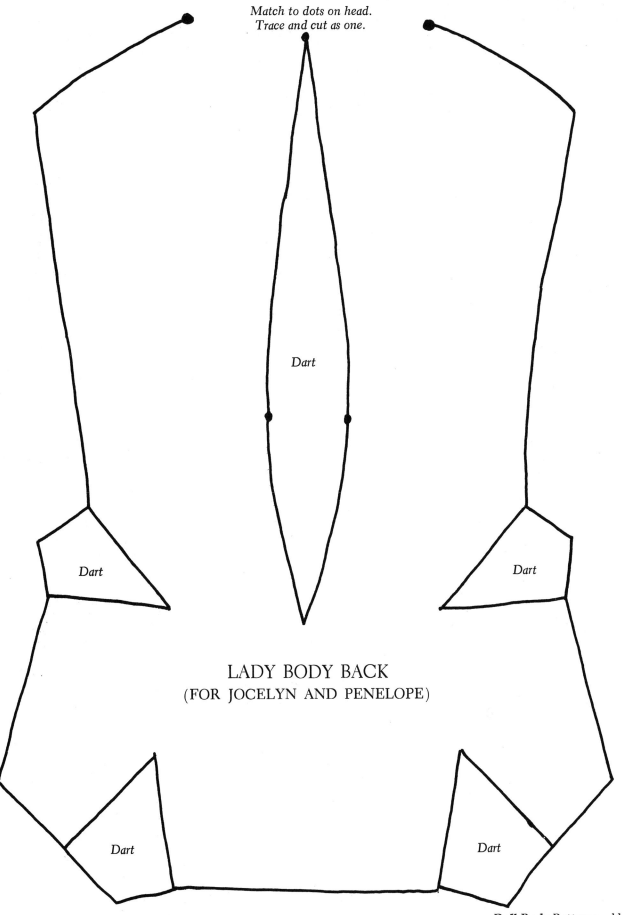

ALLOW FOR ALL SEAMS WHEN CUTTING

Match to dots on head.
Trace and cut as one.

Dart

Dart

Dart

LADY BODY BACK
(FOR JOCELYN AND PENELOPE)

Dart

Dart

Underwear Patterns

Panties

MATERIALS

FABRIC

¼ yard white batiste

NOTIONS AND TRIMMINGS

½ yard ¼″ elastic
1 yard lace trimming (*optional*)

1. Make hems at leg edges and insert elastic. Secure elastic at both ends.
2. Sew leg seams on each piece. (*See diagram*)
3. Turn one piece right side out and insert inside other piece, matching leg seams.
4. Sew both center backs to both center fronts in one continuous seam.
5. Turn right side out.
6. Sew casing at waist edge, leaving about ½″ to insert elastic. Cut elastic to doll's waist measure and insert.
7. Trim if you wish.

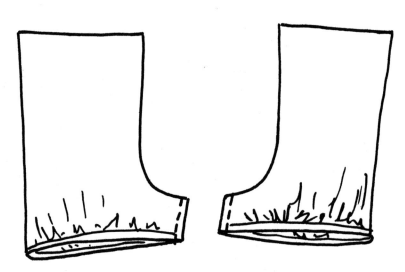

Sewing Leg Seams

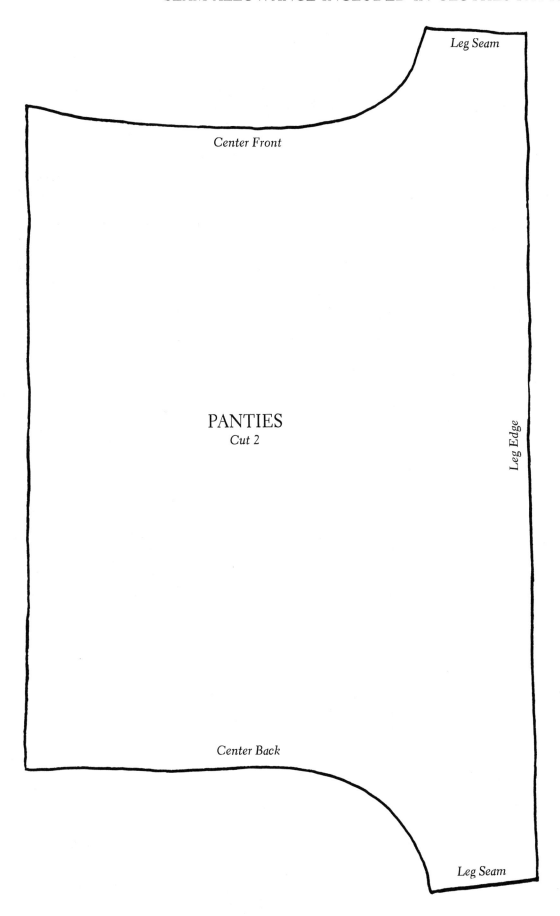

Leg Seam

Center Front

PANTIES
Cut 2

Leg Edge

Center Back

Leg Seam

Pantalettes

MATERIALS

FABRIC

½ yard white batiste or eyelet

NOTIONS AND TRIMMINGS

½ yard ¼″ elastic
1¼ yards insertion lace
1¼ yards 1½″ eyelet ruffling

Knee Length Pantalettes

1. Cut pattern at line indicated for knee length.
2. Hem lower leg edges with narrow, rolled hem.
3. Sew one row of eyelet ruffling at edge of hem. Cover stitches with a row of insertion lace.
4. Sew second row of eyelet ruffling above first, so that it just covers the top of insertion lace. Cover stitches with insertion lace.
5. Sew leg seams on each piece. (*See diagram, p. 14*)
6. Turn one piece right side out and insert inside other piece, matching leg seams.

7. Sew both center backs to both center fronts in one continuous seam.
8. Turn right side out.
9. Sew casing at waist edge, leaving about ½″ to insert elastic. Cut elastic to doll's waist measure and insert.
10. If you wish, omit steps 3 and 4, and make four rows of ¼″ tucks on lower legs. Press toward lower edge.

Long Length Pantalettes

1. Hem lower leg edges with ½″ hem.
2. Apply eyelet ruffling where indicated on pattern.
3. Cover stitches on eyelet ruffling with insertion lace or ribbon.
4. Sew leg seams on each piece. (*See diagram, p. 14*)
5. Turn one piece right side out and insert inside other piece, matching leg seams.
6. Sew both center backs to center fronts in one continuous seam.
7. Turn right side out.
8. Sew casing at waist edge, leaving about ½″ to insert elastic. Cut elastic to doll's waist measure and insert.

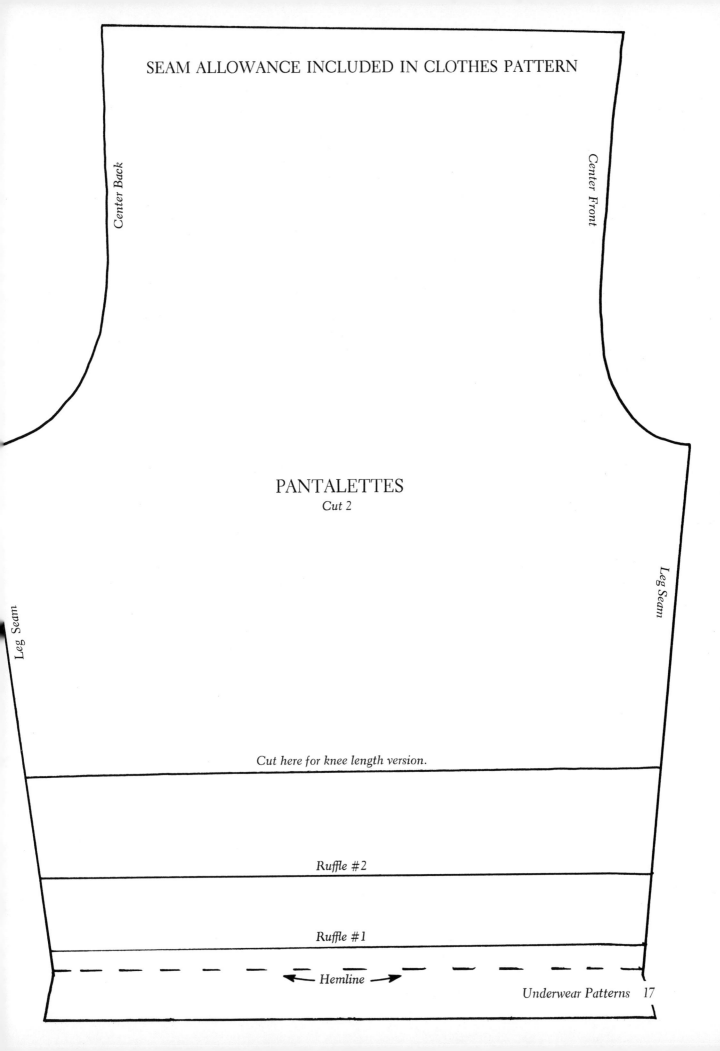

SEAM ALLOWANCE INCLUDED IN CLOTHES PATTERN

Center Back

Center Front

Leg Seam

Leg Seam

PANTALETTES
Cut 2

Cut here for knee length version.

Ruffle #2

Ruffle #1

← *Hemline* →

Chemise

MATERIALS

FABRIC

½ yard white batiste

NOTIONS AND TRIMMINGS

½ yard ¼″ elastic
1 yard 1½″ eyelet ruffling
ribbon (*optional*)

1. Sew front to back at shoulder seams.
2. Gather front neckline between dots to fit doll; secure stitches.
3. Press facings at center back to inside.

4. Finish neck edge with narrow bias strip.
5. Gather sleeves to fit armhole and sleeve binding.
6. Sew one edge of sleeve binding to lower edge of sleeve.
7. Fit upper edge of sleeve to armhole and stitch.
8. Turn binding to inside, forming piping, and hem in place.
9. Sew sleeve and side seams in one stitching.
10. Casing is optional. Sew bias binding to inside where indicated on pattern, and insert narrow tape or elastic in casing. Secure elastic at fold for facing in back.
11. Finish lower edge with eyelet ruffle.
12. Tie a ribbon at waist and sew lace ruffles on sleeves, if desired.

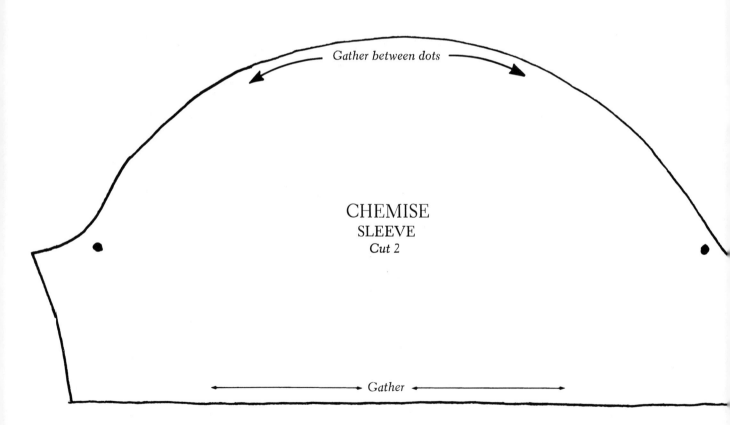

Gather between dots

CHEMISE
SLEEVE
Cut 2

Gather

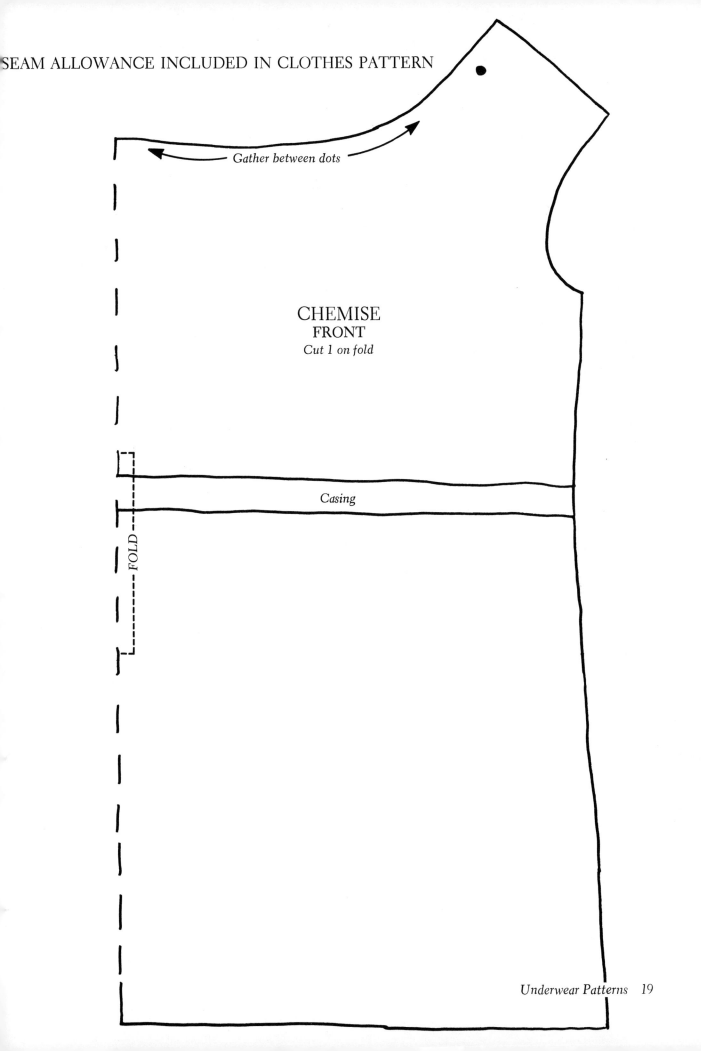

SEAM ALLOWANCE INCLUDED IN CLOTHES PATTERN

Gather between dots

CHEMISE
FRONT
Cut 1 on fold

Casing

FOLD

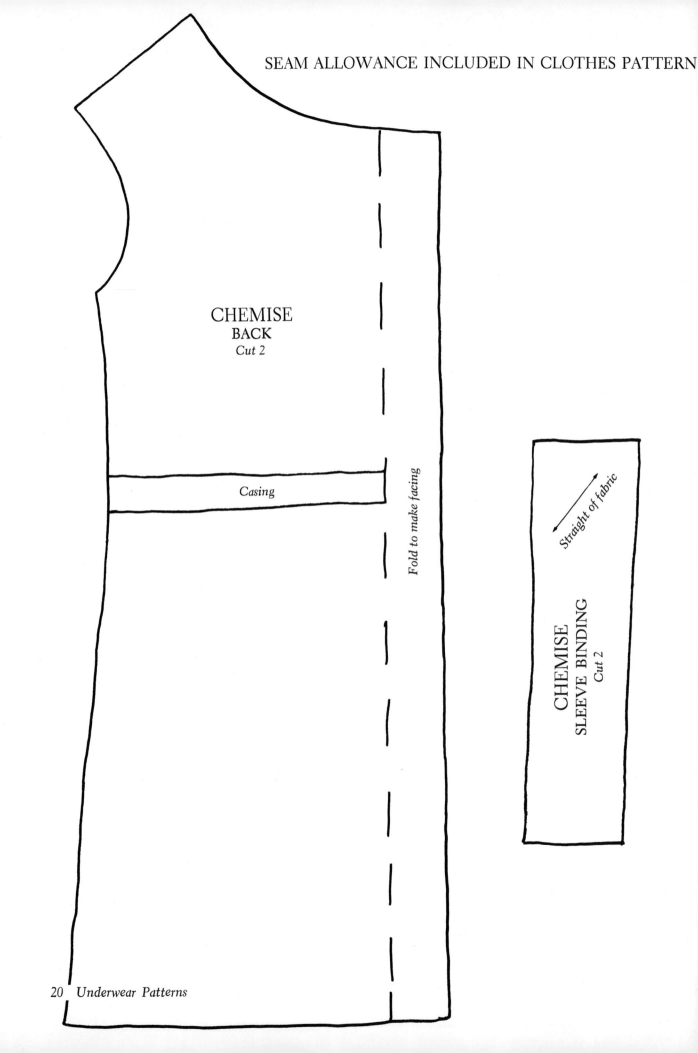

CHEMISE
BACK
Cut 2

Casing

Fold to make facing

Straight of fabric

CHEMISE
SLEEVE BINDING
Cut 2

Corset

MATERIALS

FABRIC

¼ yard pink or white slipper satin

NOTIONS AND TRIMMINGS

1 pair baby shoelaces
1 yard feather boning

1. Cut eight pieces: 2 sets of backs and fronts for corset and 2 sets of backs and fronts for corset lining.

2. Fold darts along solid lines; stitch along dotted lines.

3. Sew the four sets together along notched edges (2 *corsets and 2 linings*).

4. Stitch feather boning to the two lining sets, along dart seams and side seams.

5. Press up ¼″ along lower edges of lining and corset.

6. Right sides together, sew corsets and linings together, leaving open at lower (*pressed*) edges for turning. Trim away boning from seam allowances, if necessary. Turn right sides out.

7. Slip stitch lower edges closed.

8. To make lacing holes in both front and back of each piece, put in eyelets along straight edges where indicated with the eyelet attachment for your sewing machine or with an awl.

9. Lace front as you would a shoe from top to bottom. Put on doll and lace the back, pulling in the waist for an "hourglass" figure as you lace. Baby shoelaces are excellent for lacing.

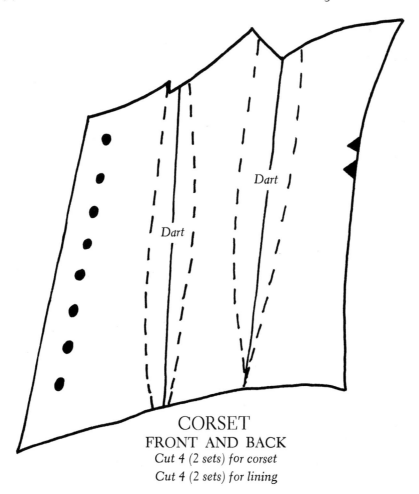

CORSET
FRONT AND BACK
Cut 4 (2 sets) for corset
Cut 4 (2 sets) for lining

Bustle Shaper

MATERIALS

FABRIC

5½″ × 5½″ piece of fabric

NOTIONS AND TRIMMINGS

¼″ ribbon
Stuffing

1. Fold fabric in half and sew along one long side. Turn right side out.
2. Measure down 2¼″ from one short edge and stitch across.
3. Lightly stuff both ends and slip stitch openings.
4. Stitch ribbon over stitching at 2¼″ point. Tie around doll's waist. Bustle is worn over corset and under petticoat. Ribbon should be long enough to tie around doll's waist.

Bust Shaper

MATERIALS

FABRIC

10″ × 10″ white cotton

NOTIONS AND TRIMMINGS

Ruffled lace
Ribbon

1. Cut four. Sew darts.
2. Right sides together, sew two pairs together, turning one dart one way and the other the opposite way to avoid bulk. Leave an opening to turn.
3. Turn to right side.
4. Cover with circles of ruffled lace.
5. Cut lengths of ribbon for shoulder straps.
6. Sew lengths of ribbon at lower sides of lace circles, which are long enough to go around doll and tie in a bow.
7. Sew shoulder straps to lace circles at tops, then sew to ribbon on back.

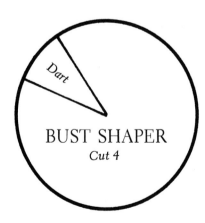

BUST SHAPER
Cut 4

SEAM ALLOWANCE INCLUDED IN CLOTHES PATTERN

The Dolls

24 *Josephine*

Josephine, 1820's

Josephine is fashioned after wooden dolls popular at this time. These dolls were rather crude with no attempt at realism. The faces which resembled medieval portraits were painted on a round knob of a head. Our cloth version wears a shawl, which was the rage at this time. She can wear a chemise, made of the same fabric as the dress, but she would wear no panties as they had not yet been invented.

MATERIALS

FABRICS

BODY
⅓ yard skin color

DRESS
½ yard voile or batiste, printed with tiny flowers

SLIPPERS
5″ × 10″ piece of satin, to match dress
5″ × 10″ piece of interfacing

UNDERWEAR
For underwear materials, see pages 14-22.

NOTIONS AND TRIMMINGS

BODY
Embroidery threads: shaded pink, medium blue, medium-dark brown, skin color (*slightly deeper than body fabric*) black, white
2 ounces medium-brown yarn (*for hair*)

DRESS
1 yard ¾″ velvet ribbon (*to match dress*)
½ yard ¼″ lace (*for sleeves*)
Snaps
Triangle of lace, silk, crochet or tatting (*for shawl*)

SLIPPERS
1¼ yards ¼″ ribbon to match satin
Cardboard

OPTIONAL
Tiny beads, strung into long rope with tassels at both ends
Pair of small earrings for pierced ears

JOSEPHINE'S EARS

Right sides together, stitch around longer curved edge

of ears. Turn right side out. Stitch darts on front of head. Right sides facing, stitch ears to front of head at dots.

JOSEPHINE'S FACE

For nose, use one strand of embroidery thread in a deeper shade of the skin color. Use tiny outline stitch. Do eyebrow and nose in a continuous line. Then with one strand of medium-dark brown, make another line of stitching for eyebrow directly above other stitches, only along the eyebrow. Use one strand for lines below nose and for chin in the skin color. Use three strands for the rest of face. Fill in eyelid with extra rows of outline stitch. Cheeks and mouth are done with shaded pink satin stitch, irises with medium blue satin or close buttonhole stitch, eye outline with medium-dark brown. Lightly shade along both sides of nose with brown colored pencil.

JOSEPHINE'S HAIR

Cut about three yards of yarn. Wet thoroughly, and wrap around a knitting needle and allow to dry. Meanwhile, thread a large-eyed needle with two strands of yarn. Following hairline, cover head with large back stitches—each stitch can be one inch or more long. Stagger the stitches, and keep the rows close enough together so that the scalp does not show through. The

Back Stitch

front hairline should be sewn to give the suggestion of a center part; the rest of hair should be sewn to look as though it is all pulled to the top of the head.

Using 15 strands of yarn, make a long braid and sew to top of head in the shape of a crown.

When yarn on knitting needle is dry, cut short lengths (about ten coils). Fold the coils in half to make two curls. Sew these curls all around hairline, trimming where necessary so that they don't hang in the doll's eyes.

JOSEPHINE'S COSTUME

UNDERWEAR

1. Although women of the period did not wear panties, if you wish doll to be less naked, use the knee-length version of the pantalettes cut of white batiste on page 16.

2. Use chemise on page 18.

DRESS

1. Run gathering stitches where indicated on front bodice, back bodice and sleeves.

2. Sew shoulder seams, press open.

3. Measure doll's arms just above elbow. Add ¾" to this measurement, and cut a strip of self bias. Pull up gathers in lower sleeve to fit bias strip. Stitch self bias strip to lower sleeve. Trim seam to just less than ⅛".

4. Pull up gathers in upper sleeve to fit armhole. Stitch sleeve to armhole.

5. Open out bias strips on sleeves, and stitch bias, sleeve and side seam of bodice in one continuous stitching.

6. Turn sleeve bias strips to inside and hem in place. The binding should be no wider than ⅛" on right side. Trim if necessary before hemming.

7. Fold in back facings and finish neck edge with self bias strip. It may be helpful to try the dress on doll at this point to be sure the gathers at neck and "waistline" fit properly and are distributed evenly. Secure the gathering stitches by threading them in a needle and taking a couple of tiny stitches.

8. Cut the ½ yard of lace for sleeves into two equal pieces. Fold each in half and sew tiny French seams to finish raw ends. Run gathering stitches in the top of lace and pull up to fit armhole. Tack securely inside sleeve, over bias hem.

9. Cut a piece of dress fabric 12" × 19". Gather to fit bodice. Skirt should be barely gathered in front, with most of the fullness at center back. Open out facings on back bodice and sew skirt to bodice.

10. Sew a ⅝" seam in center back skirt to within 2" of waistline. Press seam open, and hem entire back opening. Close with snaps.

11. Hem skirt so that it falls about ¾" above ankle.

SLIPPERS

1. Cut uppers of interfacing and press on wrong side of satin before cutting the satin.

2. Cut out satin uppers.

3. Sew center back seam in uppers.

4. Run a row of tiny stay stitches on seamline around instep. Clip at center front, turn to inside, and hem in place.

5. Cut a pair of soles out of interfacing (*no seam allowance*). Press to wrong side of satin before cutting satin. After pressing, cut satin soles with a ¼" seam allowance.

6. Stitch sole to upper.

7. Cut a pair of innersoles (*no seam allowance*) out of cardboard. Use the sole pattern, and cut slightly inside the seamline. Glue the innersoles to wrong side of satin. When dry, cut out satin (*no seam allowance*) and slip innersoles inside shoes.

8. With an awl, pierce holes at dots in uppers. With a large eyed needle, thread ribbon through these holes. Tie on doll's foot like ballet slippers.

FINISHING TOUCHES

1. Tie on waist ribbon with bow at side front.

2. Drape shawl over one arm.

3. If desired, decorate with beads and earrings. Beads should be long enough to drape from front neck, around neck, with both ends dangling in front. The beads have no clasp.

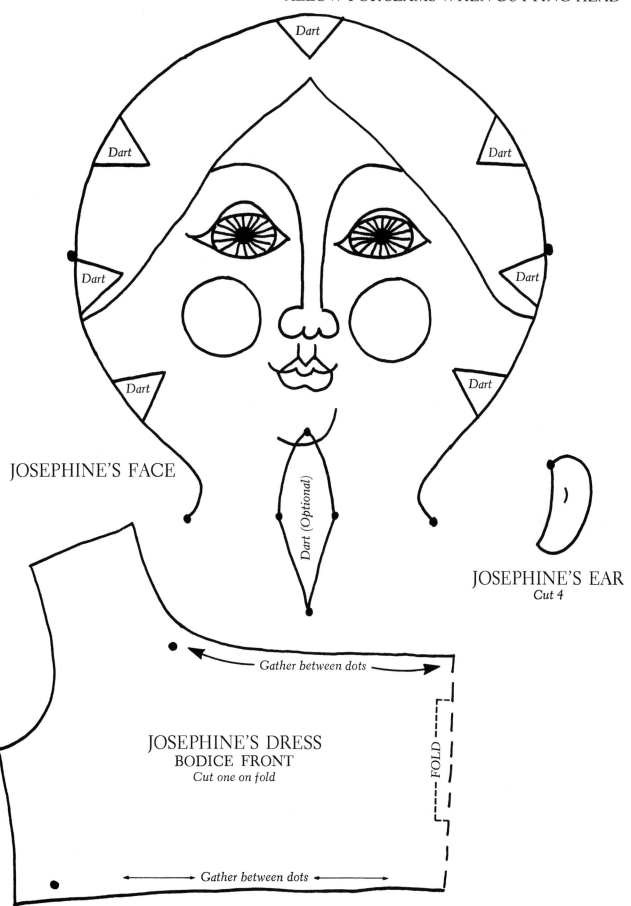

Dart

Dart

Dart

Dart

Dart

Dart

Dart

Dart

JOSEPHINE'S FACE

Dart (Optional)

JOSEPHINE'S EAR
Cut 4

Gather between dots

JOSEPHINE'S DRESS
BODICE FRONT
Cut one on fold

FOLD

Gather between dots

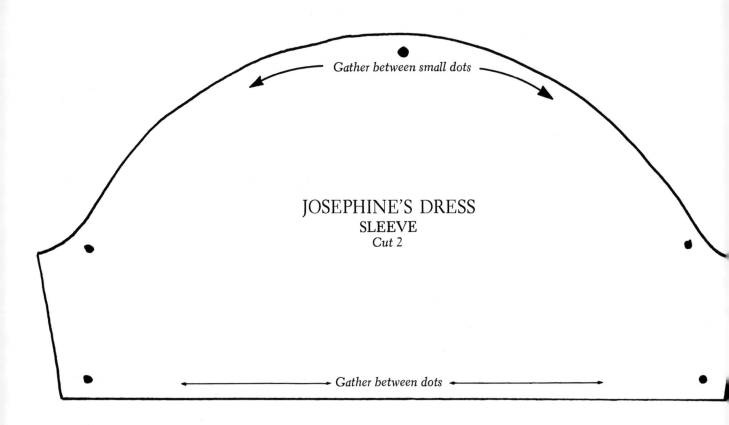

Gather between small dots

JOSEPHINE'S DRESS
SLEEVE
Cut 2

Gather between dots

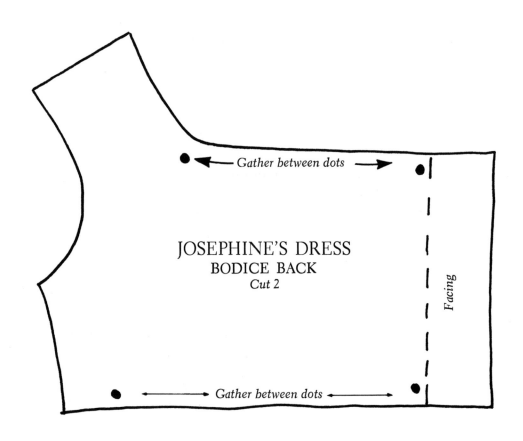

Gather between dots

JOSEPHINE'S DRESS
BODICE BACK
Cut 2

Facing

Gather between dots

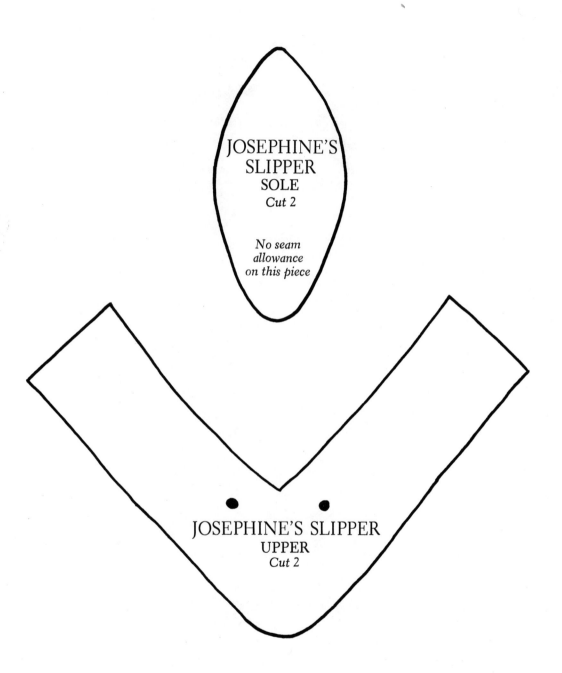

JOSEPHINE'S
SLIPPER
SOLE
Cut 2

*No seam
allowance
on this piece*

JOSEPHINE'S SLIPPER
UPPER
Cut 2

30 *Victoria*

Victoria, 1830's

Victoria was inspired by a French paper doll printed in 1832. Her walking coat and hat are made of velvet, trimmed with ermine. She sports an ostrich feather in her hat. The costume is completed with the tight-fitting leggings which were worn during this period over black shoes.

MATERIALS

FABRICS

BODY
⅓ yard skin color

COAT AND HAT
1 yard lightweight, drapeable velveteen (*red, wine or sky blue*)
⅓ yard lining fabric (*same color as velveteen*)
⅓ yard interfacing

LEGGINGS
⅛ yard grey cotton suede
Scrap of black cotton

UNDERWEAR
For underwear materials, see pages 14-22.

NOTIONS AND TRIMMINGS

BODY
Embroidery threads: white, black, blue, medium brown, shaded pink, skin color or slightly deeper shade
2 ounces medium-brown yarn (*for hair*)

COAT AND HAT
1 yard white, short-haired fake fur (*4″ wide*)
Black, fluffy feathers (*mine were maribou from my husband's tackle box*)
Black indelible marking pen (*felt tip*)
1 yard black grosgrain ribbon (*¼″ wide*)

OPTIONAL
8 6mm black round beads or buttons

VICTORIA'S FACE

1. With one strand of beige embroidery thread, embroider brows with tiny, single stitches, to give a natural looking brow.
2. Outline chin with two strands of embroidery thread the same shade as the "skin." The original doll was done in a fleshy peach color, with the embroidery thread a shade darker.
3. Embroider irises in medium blue, using three strands and either close buttonhole stitch or satin stitch.
4. Pupils are satin stitches with three strands of black. Outline eyes with two strands of the same shade as eyebrows.
5. Use two strands of beige and satin stitch for nostrils.
6. Use three strands of shaded pink and satin stitch for mouth.
7. If you wish, you can make face look three-dimensional by shading inner eye and sides of nose *lightly* with brown colored pencil, and rouging cheeks with pink colored pencil.

VICTORIA'S HAIR

1. With four 24-inch strands, make a twisted cord. Tie ends together to secure. Arrange cord into four or five "curls."
2. Starting at location of lowest dart on head, sew "curls" around head, working just above hairline.
3. With crewel needle and one strand of yarn, embroider hairline around face. Use outline stitch. Your stitches can be ¾″ or longer. The crewel needle is thin enough that it will not make holes in the fabric.
4. With larger needle and two strands of yarn, cover the rest of head with large outline stitches, working down into "curls." As you come to the knots in the "curls," make a few stitches next to them and then push the knots under the stitches to conceal.

VICTORIA'S LEGS

Cut the doll's legs from grey cotton suede and the soles of the feet from the scrap of black cotton. This will give the effect of leggings over black shoes, which was the fashion for this particular outfit. If you wish you may embroider "buttons" on the sides of the leggings. Follow the pattern on page 59.

VICTORIA'S COSTUME

UNDERWEAR

Use panties on page 14 and chemise on page 18.

WALKING COAT

If you plan to use velveteen, as suggested, be sure to cut all pieces in the same direction (with nap).

CAPE

The pattern on page 37 is a guide only. The actual pattern piece is cut out of newspaper.

1. Fold the newspaper in half, and then fold again so that you have two folded edges.
2. Cut circle from the newspaper, using the guide at folded edges of newspaper.
3. Using the newspaper pattern, cut one piece from coat fabric and one piece from lining fabric. Cut the hole in the center and slash along one straight edge of the fabric on coat and lining.
4. Right sides together, sew cape to cape lining by sewing the slashed ends and outer edge of cape circles. Trim corners and turn right side out.
5. Run a gathering stitch around neck edge. Pull up gathers to match neck of jacket between dots.

BODICE

1. Sew shoulder seams.
2. Run gathering stitches in sleeves at armhole and lower edge of upper sleeve.
3. Pull up gathers to fit lower sleeves and stitch lower sleeve to upper sleeve.
4. Stitch sleeve facing to lower edge of lower sleeve.
5. Pull up gathers at armhole edge to fit armhole and stitch in place.
6. Sew sleeve and side seam of bodice in one continuous stitching.
7. Fold in front facings.
8. Attach cape to jacket by stitching ⅜" from edge through cape and jacket between dots. Clip at intervals around neck. Turn raw edges to right side and tack down.
9. From fur, cut a ¾" wide strip long enough to go around neck from dot to dot. Mark the fur with an indelible marker so that it resembles ermine. Slip stitch to neck edge over raw edges.
10. Turn remaining raw edge to inside; stitch in place.
11. Trim wrist edges of sleeves and lower edge of cape in the same way with the fur.

SKIRT

1. Cut a piece of the coat fabric 8" × 25".
2. Open the facings on the bodice and pin the top of the skirt to the bodice from front edges to side seams. This front portion of the skirt is smooth, and the remainder is gathered to fit the back of the bodice. Mark the smooth distance.
3. Unpin the skirt from the bodice and gather the back portion to fit between the notches snugly. Secure ends.
4. Stitch skirt to bodice, right sides together. Fold in facings on front edges and blind hem in place. Sew a hook and eye at waist in front. (This will be concealed by the belt.)
5. Turn up ¾" at lower edge and hem. Trim with remaining piece of fur.
6. The skirt can be lined to give it a nice finish.

HAT

The pattern on page 37 is a guide only. The actual pattern piece is cut out of newspaper.

1. Following the instructions given for the cape, cut two pieces with center hole of coat fabric for the brim and brim facing of the hat. Cut one piece of coat fabric without center hole and one piece of lining fabric without center hole for the crown of the hat.
2. Cut one piece with center hole from interfacing.
3. Stitch interfacing to brim facing along outer edge. Trim interfacing very close to stitching. Cut away seam allowance of interfacing at inner edge.
4. Using first stitching as a guide, with right sides facing, stitch brim to brim facing along outer edge. Trim and turn right side out. Stitch around crown and clip at intervals all around.
5. Sewing fabric and lining as one, run a gathering stitch around the crown. Pull up to fit brim and stitch to brim.
6. Stitch ribbon over raw edges on inside and tack to crown to hide raw edge.
7. Fold up brim in front at an angle and tack to crown to hold in place. Add feathers. You may want to stuff tissue inside the crown to help it hold its shape on doll's head.

FINISHING TOUCHES

1. If desired, sew beads or buttons on each side of front closing. Make "frog" loops with black embroidery thread as follows: crochet a chain one inch long. Slip stitch in first stitch to form circle. End off. Twist once in center to form two loops. Sew to front edge between buttons. Close.
2. Tie black ribbon at waist, with bow at right side.

VICTORIA'S FACE

SEAM ALLOWANCE INCLUDED IN CLOTHES PATTERN

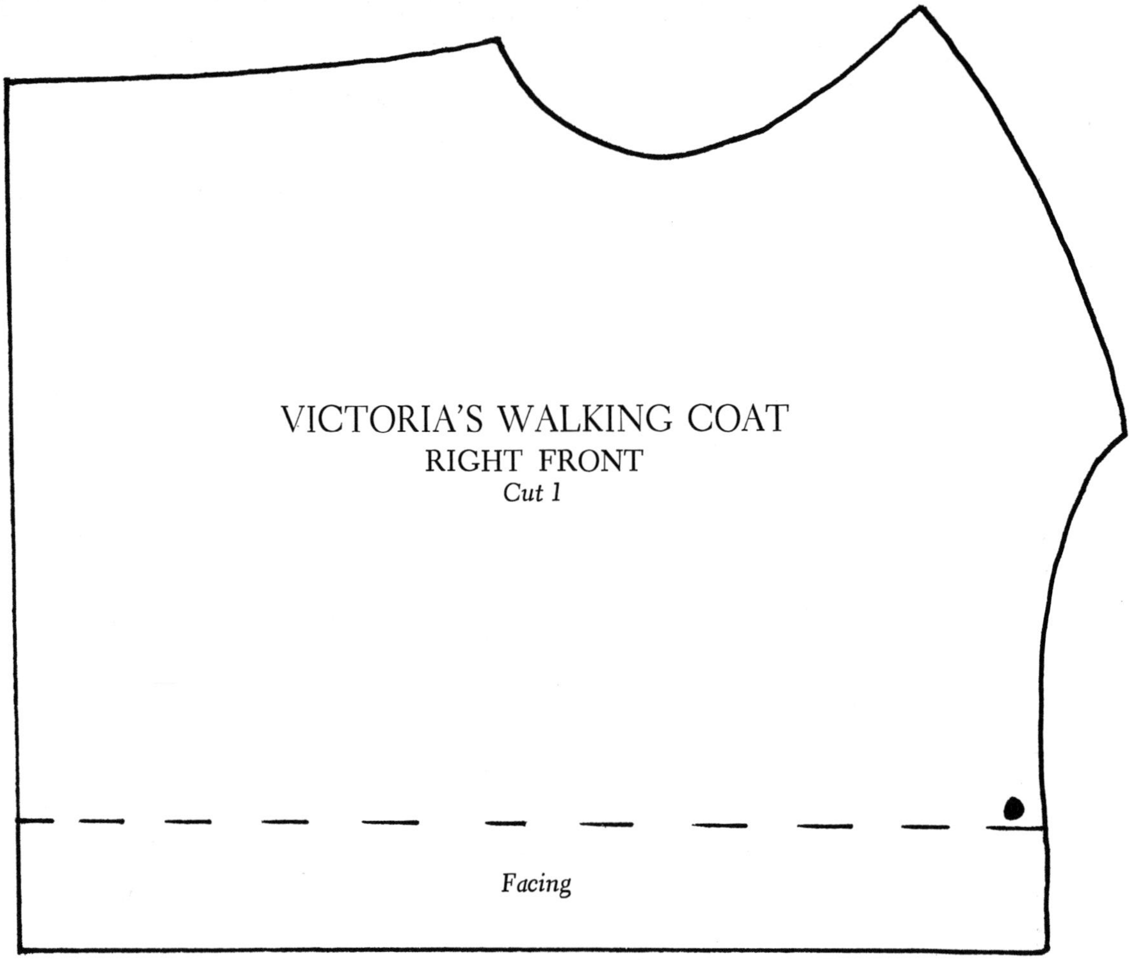
VICTORIA'S WALKING COAT
RIGHT FRONT
Cut 1
Facing

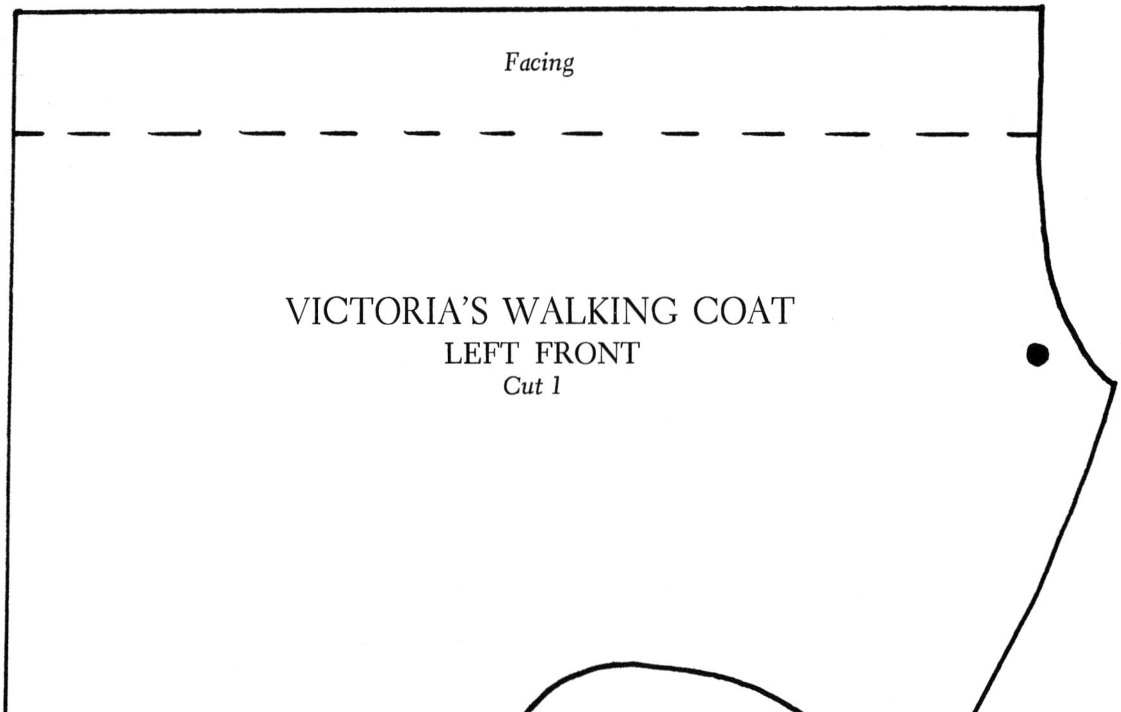
Facing
VICTORIA'S WALKING COAT
LEFT FRONT
Cut 1

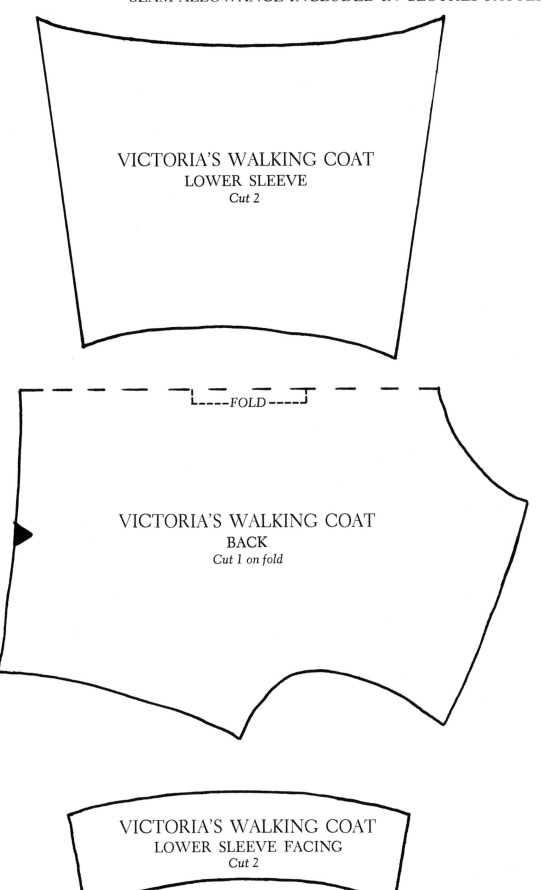

VICTORIA'S WALKING COAT
LOWER SLEEVE
Cut 2

FOLD

VICTORIA'S WALKING COAT
BACK
Cut 1 on fold

VICTORIA'S WALKING COAT
LOWER SLEEVE FACING
Cut 2

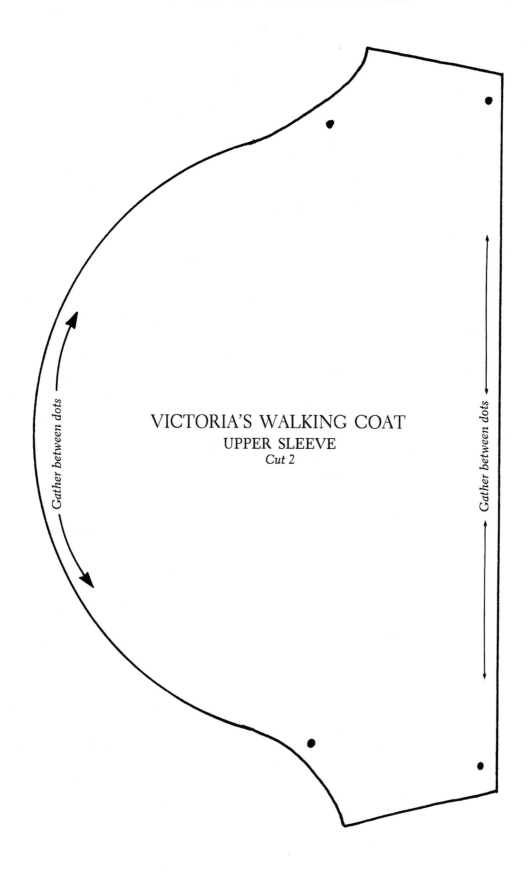

VICTORIA'S WALKING COAT
UPPER SLEEVE
Cut 2

Gather between dots

Gather between dots

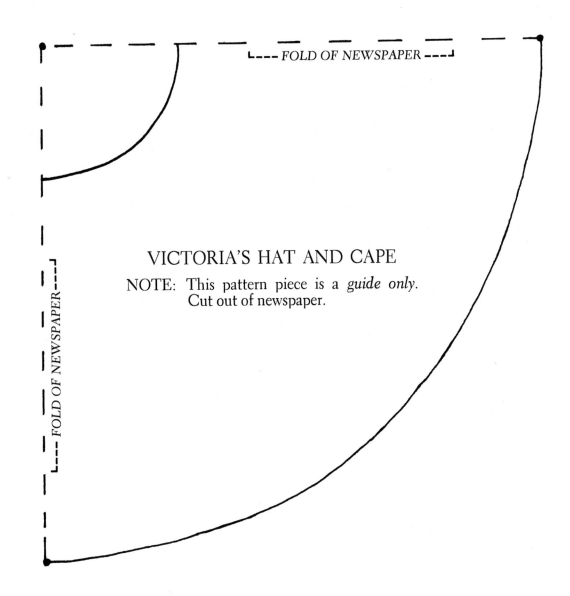

FOLD OF NEWSPAPER

FOLD OF NEWSPAPER

VICTORIA'S HAT AND CAPE

NOTE: This pattern piece is a *guide only*.
Cut out of newspaper.

38 *Mistress Black*

Mistress Black, 1830's

The inspiration for Mistress Black's clothes came from the same paper doll as Victoria. She was made black so that there would be a doll in the collection representing each ethnic group. In this way you can enlarge your collection with your own dress designs representing many nationalities throughout the world.

MATERIALS

FABRICS

BODY
⅓ yard cocoa fabric

DRESS AND HAT
½ yard plain colored taffeta, silk or sheer cotton

PINAFORE AND HAT
¾ yard white batiste or eyelet

SHOES
5″ × 10″ piece of glove weight leather or felt

UNDERWEAR
For underwear materials, see pages 14-22.

NOTIONS AND TRIMMINGS

BODY
Embroidery threads: light brown, black, white, shaded pink
2 ounces black yarn (for hair)

DRESS
½ yard 1½″ wide lace (for sleeves)

PINAFORE
1 yard ¾″ ribbon (for sash)

HAT
½ yard eyelet lace or ribbon

MISTRESS BLACK'S FACE

The whites of the eyes should be painted or embroidered to make them stand out. If you plan to paint the whites of the eyes, do this first. If you would rather embroider the whites, do it after completing the irises.

Entire face is done with three strands of embroidery floss. Begin with the irises, using either close buttonhole or satin stitch. Then do the pupils. Outline the eye with black and do eyebrows. Nose can be done with either black or pink. Two short, straight stitches will do the trick. Mouth is done with shaded pink. Outline lips first with outline stitch, then do satin stitch over the outline stitches. Highlight eyes with white and rouge cheeks with colored pencil.

MISTRESS BLACK'S HAIR

If you crochet, the easiest way to make the hair is to crochet a cap of loop stitch. Using black yarn (two strands) and size F hook, chain 3, slip st in first st to form ring. Loop yarn around finger and sc in next st, increasing stitches as needed to form a slightly cupped circle. Try to keep loops fairly uniform in size. Continue working loop stitch, increasing where necessary, until cap measures approximately 5 inches. Cap should be tight on doll's head, and stretched into position, following guide lines on front head pattern. Sew to doll's head with matching thread, following hairline guide.

OPTIONAL METHODS FOR DOING THE HAIR

1. Embroider French knots all over head. This is very effective, but does not have the fullness achieved by other methods.

2. Do turkey work all over the head. This is an embroidery stitch done as follows: From right side of fabric, take a stitch, leaving an end. Make a back stitch. Next, make a back stitch, but loop the yarn over your finger to form a loop. Hold the loop on your finger until you take another back stitch to lock it. In other words, every other stitch is looped over your finger and locked in by the next back stitch. See page 40.

3. Use a piece of curly fake fur. (Real fur will attract moths.)

4. Measure doll's head and order an "Afro" wig from one of the many doll supply houses.

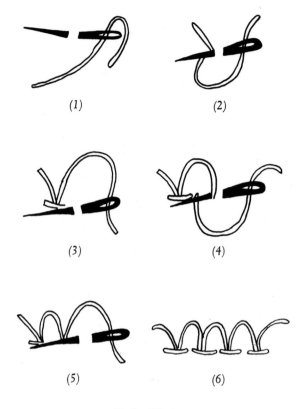

(1)　　　　　(2)

(3)　　　　　(4)

(5)　　　　　(6)

Turkey Work

MISTRESS BLACK'S COSTUME

UNDERWEAR

Use panties on page 14 and chemise on page 18.

DRESS

1. Gather front bodice neckline to size of guide. Secure gathering stitches.
2. Sew backs to front at shoulder. Press back facing to inside. Finish neck edge with narrow self fabric bias.
3. Gather top and lower edges of sleeve. Pull up gathers at lower edge to size of sleeve band. Stitch one edge of sleeve band to sleeve. Pull up gathers at top of sleeve to fit armhole. Stitch sleeve to armhole. Sew sleeve and side seams of bodice in one continuous stitching.
4. Cut skirt 12½″ × 24″. Turn in a tiny edge at each short end and press. This will give you a finished placket when back seam is sewn. Gather one long edge to fit bodice. Open out facing on bodice and sew bodice to skirt. Sew a ⅝″ seam in back skirt to within 2″ of waist. Fold seam allowance to inside, press and blind hem for back facing.
5. Hem sleeve bands and skirt. Sew snaps in back. Sew 1½″ lace ruffle to inside of sleeve band.

PINAFORE

1. Cut pinafore of batiste or eyelet. Do not use a crisp or heavy fabric; the ruffle will be too thick and stiff.
2. Sew shoulder seams in pinafore bodice. Sew one edge of narrow self bias strip to armholes. Sew side seams. Turn bias at armholes to inside and hem in place.
3. Join circles for ruffle with tiny French seam. Roll hem outer edge and short ends (*back*), or finish these edges with narrow lace. Gather ruffle to fit neck edge of pinafore, starting and stopping the ruffle at dots on pinafore back.
4. Fold in facings at center back and stitch ruffle to bodice. Finish neck edge with narrow self bias strip.
5. Cut apron 12½″ × 24″. Finish lower edge with ½″ hem. Finish side (*short*) edges with ¼″ hem or rolled hem. Gather top to fit bodice of pinafore. Sew skirt to bodice of pinafore. Finish raw edge with piece of ribbon or seam binding on inside.

HAT

The pattern on page 45 is a *guide only*. The actual pattern piece is cut out of newspaper.

1. Fold the newspaper in half, and then fold again, so that you have two folded edges.
2. Cut the circle from the newspaper, using the guide at folded edges of the newspaper.
3. Using the newspaper pattern, cut two circles of dress fabric and one of pinafore fabric.
4. Right sides together, seam the circles of dress fabric together, leaving an opening to turn. Turn and press; slip stitch opening.
5. Make a rolled hem on pinafore fabric circle, or finish with narrow lace.
6. Place circles together, pinafore fabric on top. Through all thicknesses run two rows of gathering stitches along the gathering line.
7. Pull up gathers to fit doll's head, and secure the gathering threads by threading them in a needle and ending them off. Cover gathering stitches with eyelet lace or ribbon sewn over the gathers. You may add tiny flowers if you wish.

SHOES

1. Right sides together join shoe uppers at center back.
2. Right sides together stitch upper to sole, placing dot at center back.
3. Trim close to stitching and turn.

FINISHING TOUCHES

1. Tie a ribbon at waist or make a sash from a piece of dress fabric 2″ × 36″.

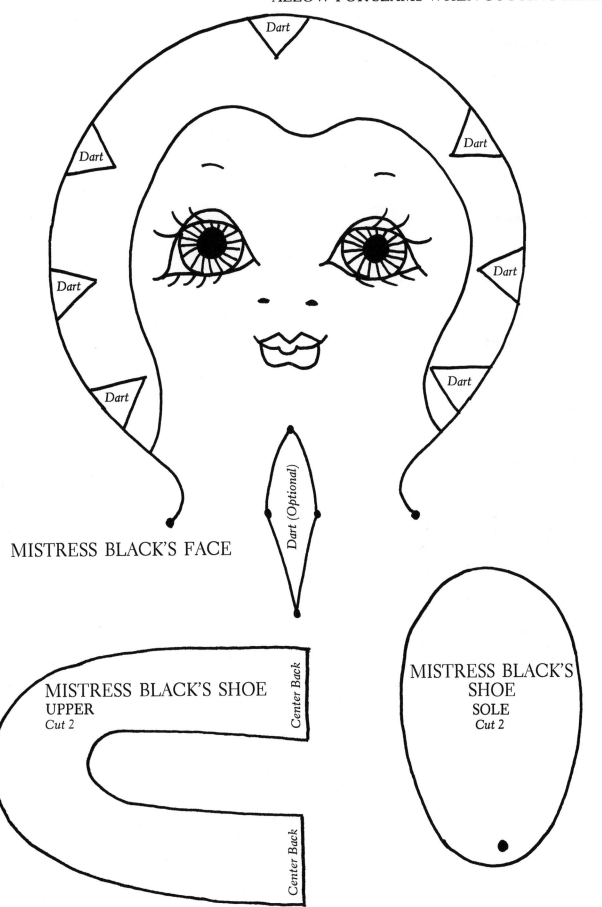

Dart

Dart

Dart

Dart

Dart

Dart

Dart (Optional)

MISTRESS BLACK'S FACE

MISTRESS BLACK'S SHOE
UPPER
Cut 2

Center Back

Center Back

MISTRESS BLACK'S
SHOE
SOLE
Cut 2

SEAM ALLOWANCE INCLUDED IN CLOTHES PATTERN

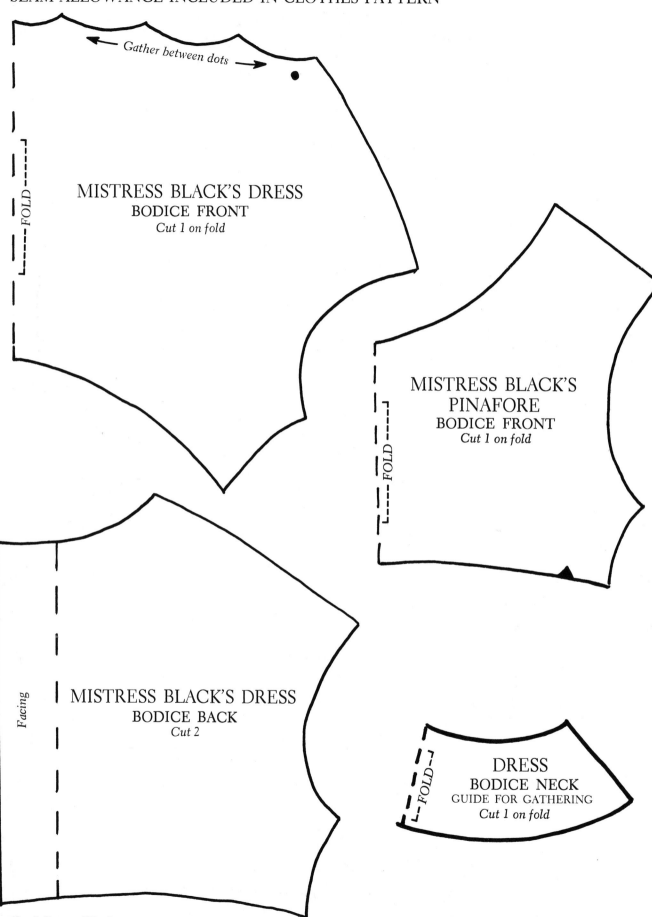

SEAM ALLOWANCE INCLUDED IN CLOTHES PATTERN

Gather between dots

FOLD

MISTRESS BLACK'S DRESS
BODICE FRONT
Cut 1 on fold

MISTRESS BLACK'S
PINAFORE
BODICE FRONT
Cut 1 on fold

FOLD

Facing

MISTRESS BLACK'S DRESS
BODICE BACK
Cut 2

FOLD

DRESS
BODICE NECK
GUIDE FOR GATHERING
Cut 1 on fold

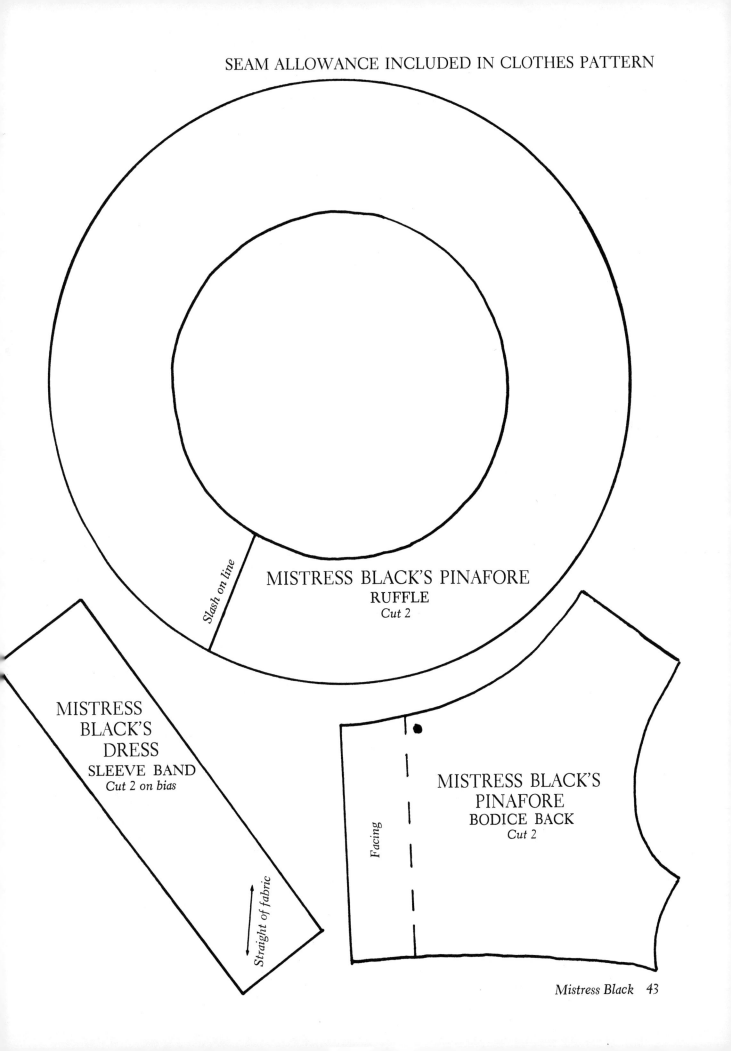

Slash on line

MISTRESS BLACK'S PINAFORE
RUFFLE
Cut 2

**MISTRESS
BLACK'S
DRESS**
SLEEVE BAND
Cut 2 on bias

Straight of fabric

Facing

**MISTRESS BLACK'S
PINAFORE**
BODICE BACK
Cut 2

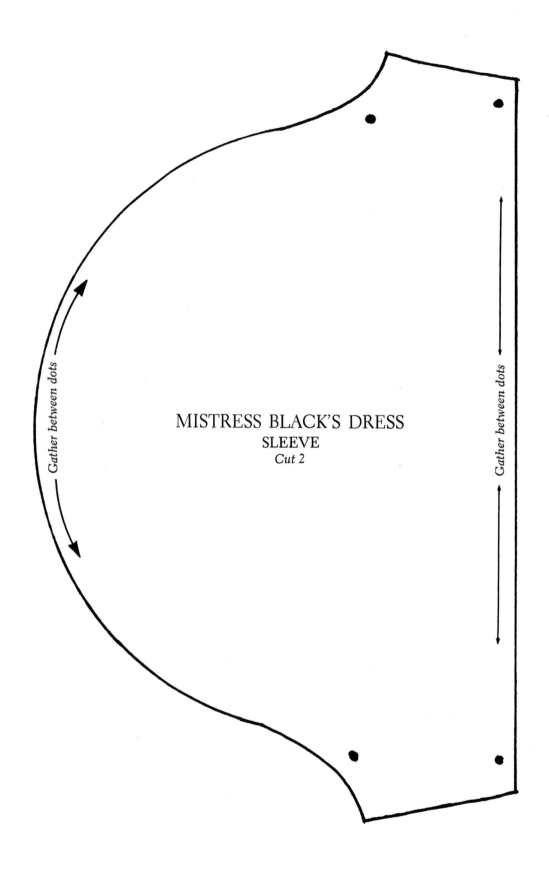

MISTRESS BLACK'S DRESS
SLEEVE
Cut 2

Gather between dots

Gather between dots

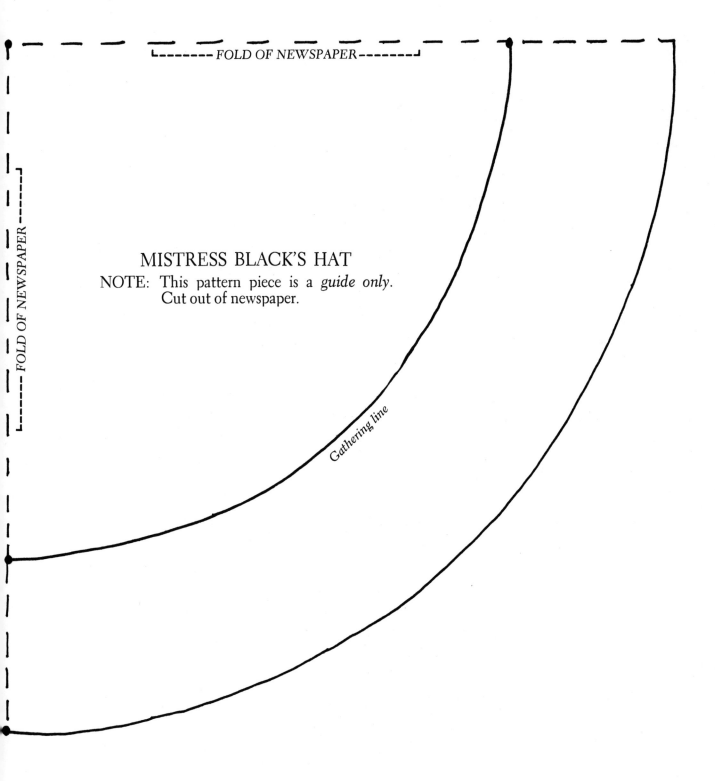

FOLD OF NEWSPAPER

FOLD OF NEWSPAPER

MISTRESS BLACK'S HAT

NOTE: This pattern piece is a *guide only*.
Cut out of newspaper.

Gathering line

Pretty Rags, 1840's

With the invention of the sewing machine (1846) clothing, especially underwear, became much more elaborate. Pantalettes, which had been ridiculed by men, were put on little girls. It was hoped this this would accustom men to seeing females in pantalettes. The pantalettes, made of muslin and lavishly trimmed with lace, eyelet and ribbon, were worn to the ankle. Pretty Rags wears a poke bonnet made of burlap to simulate straw. The bonnet is trimmed with feathers in a color to compliment her dress. The bonnet could also be trimmed with flowers or made from the same material as the dress.

MATERIALS

FABRICS

Body
⅓ yard skin color

Dress
½ yard lightweight cotton with tiny print

Hat
¼ yard straw (*or burlap*)
You can use an old straw hat or another object made of straw (*I once used a straw hot mat*)

Shoes
5″ × 10″ piece of glove leather or felt

Petticoat
½ yard white batiste

Underwear
For underwear materials, see pages 14-22.

NOTIONS AND TRIMMINGS

Body
Embroidery threads: medium brown, pink, blue, black, white
Yarn in two shades; one ounce of each shade (*for hair*)

Dress
5 tiny buttons to match dress fabric (*optional*)
Snaps

Petticoat
Hooks and eyes
1¼ yards ½″ ribbon

Hat
½ yard ½″ ribbon

Small piece grosgrain ribbon (*for straw version*)
Feathers

PRETTY RAGS'S FACE

Use three strands of embroidery thread throughout. Eyebrows, eyelashes, and outline of eye are medium brown. Irises are blue; pupils black; nose and mouth pink. It is best to do the irises first; then pupils; then outline the eye and do lashes. If desired, highlight eyes with white after eyes are completely embroidered. Rouge cheeks with pink colored pencil.

PRETTY RAGS'S HAIR

Hair is made using two shades. The original was made with pale yellow and antique gold to give the effect of sun-bleached hair.

To make sausage curls, use four 24-inch strands, two of each color. Make a twisted cord and form into three or four sausage curls. Sew securely to doll's head. Continue making cords until entire lower head is covered from just in front of where the ear would be.

Following hairline guide on pattern, and keeping a defined center part, cover head with large back stitches, working down into curls. Push knots at the ends of the twisted cords under the back stitches to conceal them. Your stitches can be ¾″ to 1″ long. Keep the rows close together to get good scalp coverage.

PRETTY RAGS'S COSTUME

UNDERWEAR

Use long length pantalettes on page 16.

PETTICOAT

1. Cut batiste 6″ by width of fabric. Seam the short ends, leaving 2¼″ opening.

2. Cut two more strips of batiste 2½″ wide by width of fabric. Seam together at short ends, forming a circle.

3. Press strip in half, so that raw edges meet. Run gathering stitches through raw edges of long edge, and pull up ruffle to fit bottom of petticoat.

4. Stitch ruffled strip to bottom of petticoat, with seam on right side. Cover seam with ½″ ribbon.

5. Cut a waistband one inch by doll's waist measure, plus one inch.

6. Gather waist of petticoat to fit waistband. Stitch to waistband.

7. Finish with hook and eye at back opening.

DRESS

1. Pin, press, and baste tucks in front bodice. Catch stitch tucks in place from wrong side with invisible stitches.

2. Sew shoulder seams.

3. Press in facings on back, and finish neck edge with narrow, self bias strip.

4. Run gathering stitches in top and lower edges of sleeves.

5. Pull up gathering at wrist edge to size of cuff. Sew one edge of cuff to sleeve.

6. Pull up gathering in top of sleeve to fit armhole. Stitch to armhole.

7. Sew side seams and sleeve seams in one continuous stitching.

8. Turn raw edge of cuff to inside and hem in place.

9. Cut skirt 11″ long by width of fabric, selvedge to selvedge. Gather one long edge to fit bodice.

10. Open out facing on bodice back and stitch skirt to bodice.

11. Seam skirt back in ⅝″ seam to within 2″ of waistline. Press seam open, and hem facing to inside.

12. Sew snaps to back opening.

13. Make a ¾″ hem in skirt. Pantalettes should show below dress.

14. Sew buttons to center front if you wish.

HAT

To make hat of straw:

1. Cut hat pieces out of cardboard (*no seam allowance*).

2. Sew first row of straw to cardboard with large whip stitches (*these stitches will be released when cardboard is completely covered*).

3. Using slip stitch, sew row after row of straw to previous row until the cardboard piece is covered, covering hat back and hat front in same manner.

4. Release whip stitches from cardboard.

5. Sew hat front around the curved edge of hat back.

6. Finish raw neck edge with small piece of grosgrain ribbon binding.

7. Attach ribbon ties and trim with feathers, flowers or bows.

OPTIONAL HAT

To make hat of burlap or dress fabric:

1. Cut two fronts and two backs of dress fabric or burlap, adding ¼″ seam allowance to pattern pieces.

2. Cut one front and one back of stiff interfacing without seam allowance.

3. Right sides together, seam fronts together along long, outside edge. Turn right side out and slip interfacing piece inside.

4. Stitch front raw edges to one back piece.

5. Run hand gathering stitches around the other back piece along curved edge. Slip interfacing piece to wrong side and pull up gathering. Press if necessary to hold in place.

6. Slip stitch to inside of hat, turning up raw edges at neck. Your hat will be completely finished, inside and out.

7. Trim same as straw.

8. If desired, the outside of the hat can be made of burlap and the inside of dress fabric.

SHOES

1. Right sides together, join shoe uppers at center back.

2. Right sides together, stitch upper to sole, placing dot at center back.

3. Trim close to stitching and turn.

4. Cut a pair of innersoles out of cardboard (*no seam allowance*) and a pair out of dress fabric (*no seam allowance*). Glue cardboard to fabric and slip inside shoes.

ALLOW FOR SEAMS WHEN CUTTING HEAD

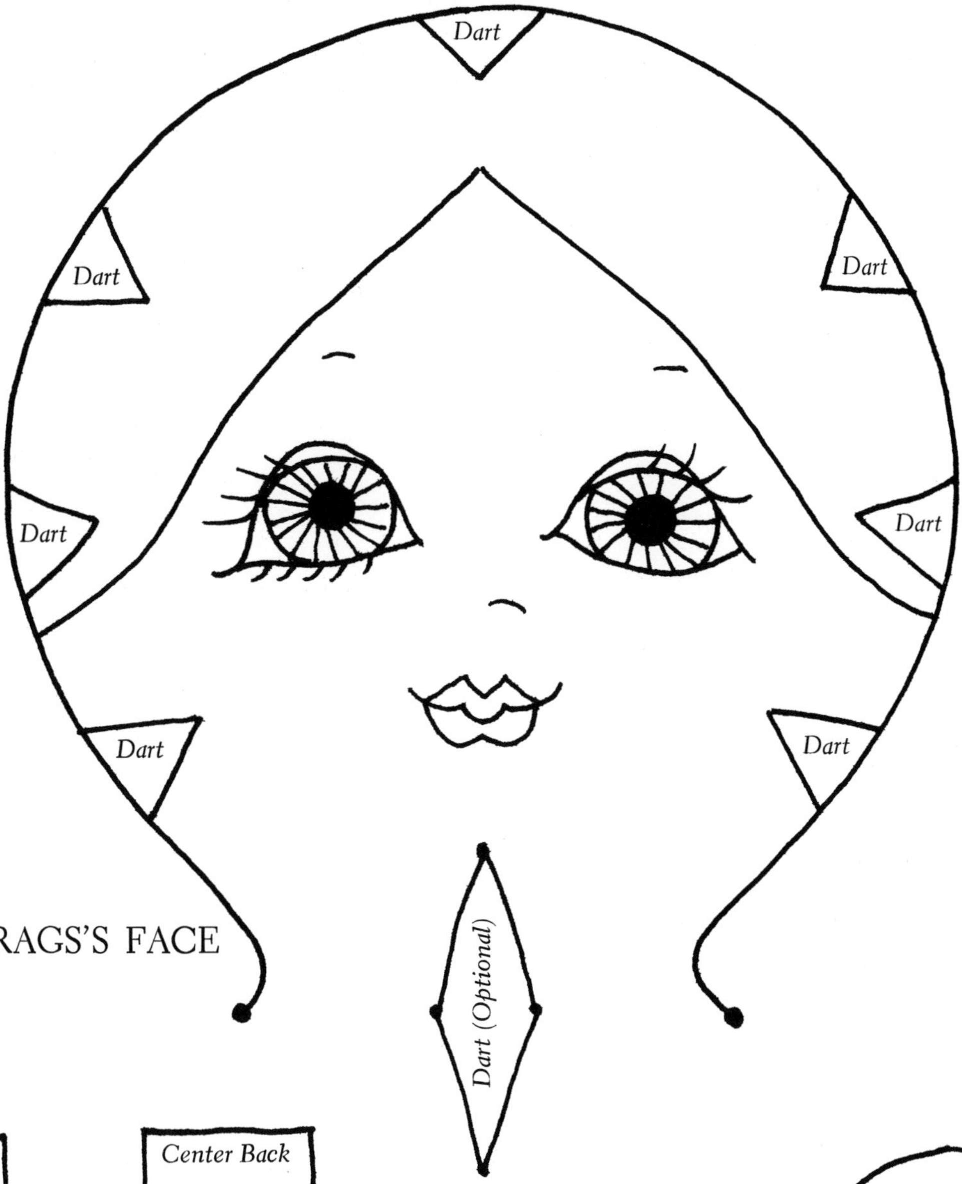
Dart
Dart
Dart
Dart
Dart
Dart
Dart
Dart (Optional)

PRETTY RAGS'S FACE

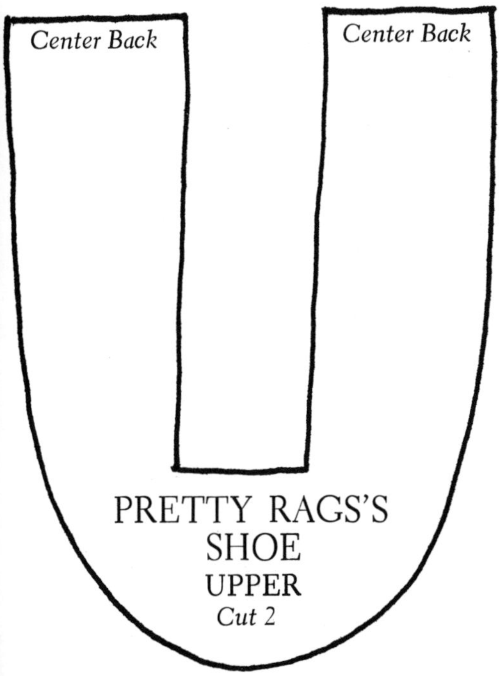
Center Back
Center Back
PRETTY RAGS'S SHOE
UPPER
Cut 2

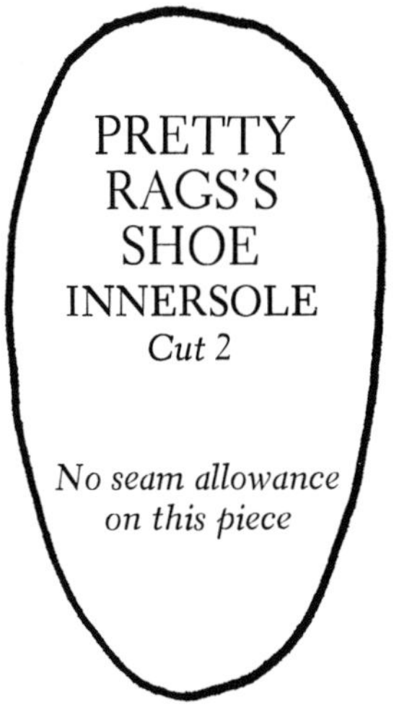
PRETTY RAGS'S SHOE
INNERSOLE
Cut 2
No seam allowance on this piece

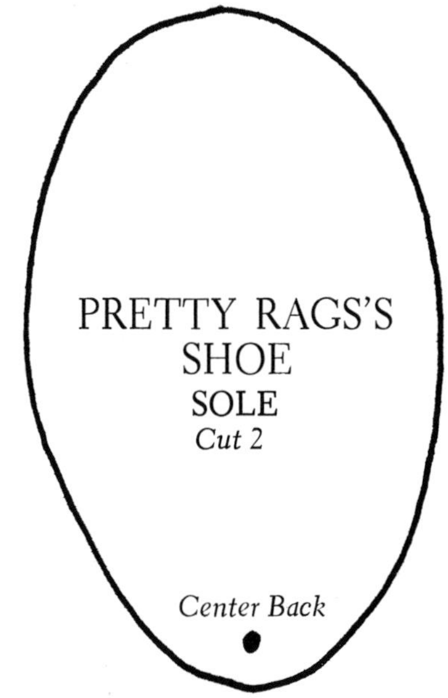
PRETTY RAGS'S SHOE
SOLE
Cut 2
Center Back

SEAM ALLOWANCE INCLUDED IN CLOTHES PATTERN

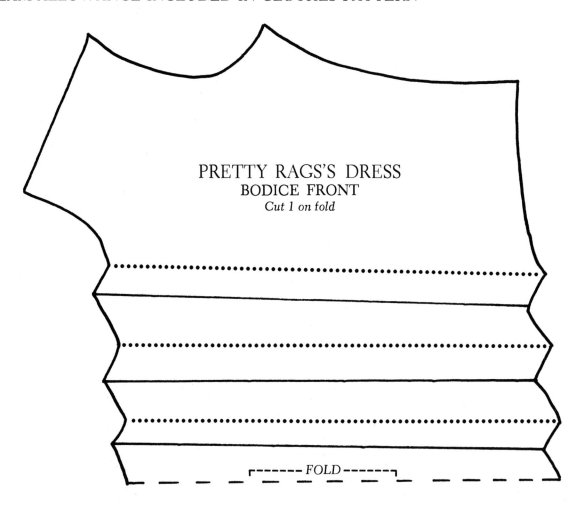

PRETTY RAGS'S DRESS
BODICE FRONT
Cut 1 on fold

┌------- FOLD ------┐

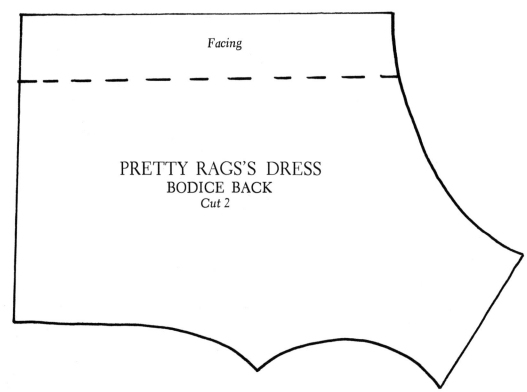

Facing

PRETTY RAGS'S DRESS
BODICE BACK
Cut 2

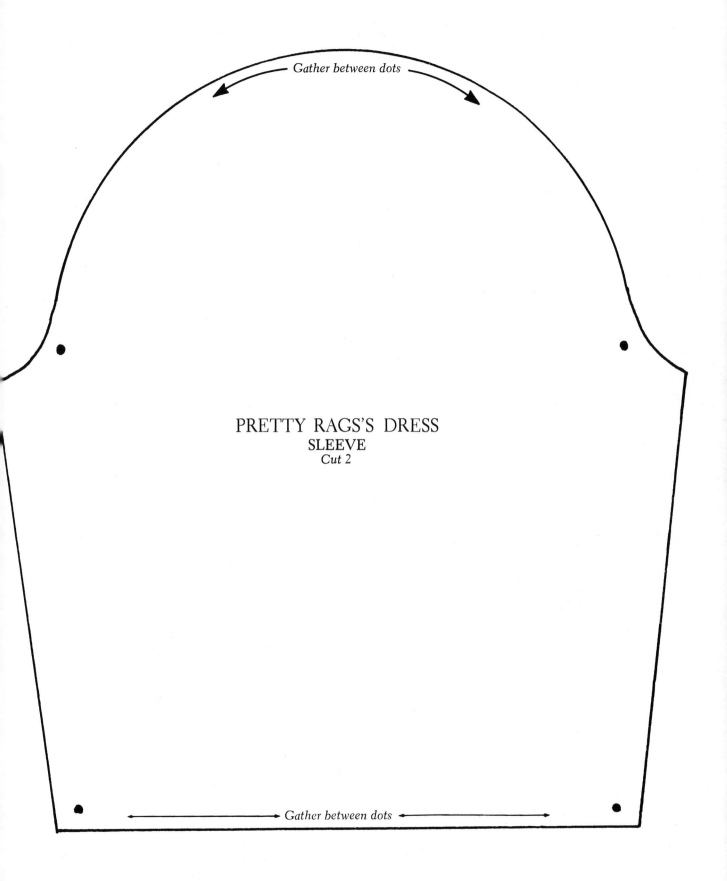

Gather between dots

PRETTY RAGS'S DRESS
SLEEVE
Cut 2

Gather between dots

PRETTY RAGS'S HAT
FRONT
Cut 1 of cardboard for straw
(no seam allowance)
or
Cut 2 of dress fabric and 1 of interfacing
(add seam allowance)
or
Cut 2 of burlap and 1 of interfacing
(add seam allowance)

PRETTY RAGS'S HAT
BACK
Cut 1 of cardboard for straw
(no seam allowance)
or
Cut 2 of dress fabric and 1 of interfacing
(add seam allowance)
or
Cut 2 of burlap and 1 of interfacing
(add seam allowance)

PRETTY RAGS'S DRESS
SLEEVE CUFF
Cut 2

54 *Melissa*

Melissa, 1850's

Except for the length of the dress, children's fashions of this period were intended to be miniature versions of their mother's. Little girls even wore corsets. Melissa's pantalettes are shorter than those worn a decade earlier, and just barely peek out below her skirt. On her feet she wears short boots. Her face is reminiscent of fashion engravings of the period, which almost always featured very heavy eyebrows and a curlicue line for the nose.

MATERIALS

FABRICS

BODY
⅓ yard skin color

DRESS
⅔ yards satin, silk, taffeta or batiste

BOOTS
5″ × 10″ piece of black cotton

UNDERWEAR
For underwear materials, see pages 14-22.

NOTIONS AND TRIMMINGS

BODY
Embroidery threads: dark brown, blue, white, black, pink, light brown
2 ounces black yarn (*for hair*)

DRESS
4 yards narrow lace edging
Flowers, ribbons (*optional*)

BOOTS
Cardboard (*for heels*)
8 small black beads for "buttons" (*optional*)

MELISSA'S FACE

Melissa's face has the heavy eyebrows and awkward curlicue nose lines characteristic of prints of the time. Her face is made three-dimensional by the use of shading above the inner eye and along the nose. Use a brown colored pencil for this.

Use one strand of light brown embroidery thread to define the nose; use three strands for the rest of the face. Eyebrows, eyelashes, and outline of the eye are medium brown. Irises are blue; pupils black and mouth pink. It is best to do the irises first; then pupils; then outline the eye and do the lashes. If desired, highlight eyes with white after eyes are embroidered. Rouge cheeks with pink colored pencil.

MELISSA'S HAIR

Cover head with turkey work, starting at center front and working from front to back in rows. Make loops about 2″ long. Trim lower edge when completed to fall just above shoulders.

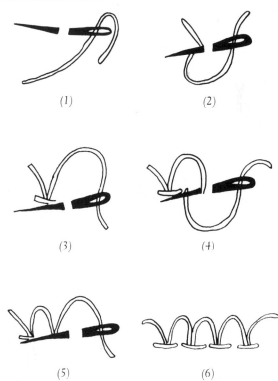

(1)   (2)

(3)   (4)

(5)   (6)

Turkey Work

An alternate method for doing the hair is to do a crocheted cap of loop stitch: Chain 4; join to form ring; 2 sc in each ch; with yarn looped around finger, sc in next st; make loops about 2″ long. Increase as necessary to form slightly capped circle, looping yarn over finger before each stitch. Make cap about 5 inches in diameter. Sew to doll's head with matching thread, stretching tight and following hairline guide.

MELISSA'S LEGS

Cut "boots" from black fabric, being sure to add seam allowances. Stay stitch upper curved edge, and carefully clip. Sew boot to upper leg, matching notches. Complete legs as described on page 2. After stuffing, embroider "closing" on outsides using an outline stitch. Sew on beads for buttons. If you wish to add heels, cut them from several layers of cardboard and glue the layers together. Paint the heels black and glue to the heels of the boots. Remember that if you do use the heels your doll will not be washable.

Optional Method: Use the regular leg pattern on page 9 and paint boots on with textile paint or waterproof markers. Add buttons and heels, as above, if desired. Use the boot portion of the leg pattern as a guide for painting.

MELISSA'S COSTUME

UNDERWEAR

Use chemise on page 18 and pantalettes on page 16, cutting at ruffle #2.

DRESS

1. Sew shoulder seams.
2. Press in back facing and finish neck edge with self bias strip.
3. Run gathering stitches on top and lower edge of sleeve.
4. Pull up gathers in lower edge of sleeve to match sleeve band and stitch one edge of sleeve band to lower edge of sleeve.
5. Pull up gathers in upper sleeve to fit armhole; stitch to armhole.
6. Sew sleeve seams and side seams in one continuous stitching.
7. Turn half of sleeve band to inside and hem.
8. Cut two pieces 4″ × 16″ for peplum. Using guide provided, round off lower edges.
9. Finish edge of peplum pieces with narrow hem. Add an edging of narrow lace.
10. Cut skirt 10½″ × 36″. Mark center of strip with tiny clip. This is the waist edge. Pin unfinished edges of peplum pieces to each side of clip, and through both thicknesses, run two rows of gathering stitches. Peplum should be about 1″ narrower than skirt at waistline in center back to allow for facing.
11. Pull up gathers to fit bodice with facings opened out. Stitch skirt to bodice.
12. Being careful not to catch in peplum, stitch a ⅝″ seam in center back skirt to within 2″ of waistline. Press seam open, and hem opening to the inside.
13. Collar is a separate piece, snapped to waistline at center front. Leaving an opening for turning in outer edge, stitch around the edges of the collar pieces. Carefully trim points and turn right side out. If your dress fabric is flimsy you may want to interface collar.
14. Trim outer edge of collar with narrow lace.
15. Tack points of collar together. Sew half of snap to under side of points and the other half to center front waistline of dress.
16. Sew snaps to back of dress.
17. Make sash 2½″ × 36″ of dress fabric. Fold in half lengthwise and sew. Turn right side out. Slip stitch ends closed. Tie on doll, with huge bow in center back.
18. Hem skirt of dress by taking two rows of tucks. Pantalettes should show below the edge of dress.
19. If desired, add flowers and ribbons at waistline.

Dart

Dart

Dart

Dart

Dart

Dart

Dart

Dart

MELISSA'S FACE

Dart (Optional)

MELISSA'S DRESS
PEPLUM
Guide for cutting lower edges

MELISSA'S DRESS
SLEEVE BAND
Cut 2

Straight of fabric

SEAM ALLOWANCE INCLUDED IN CLOTHES PATTERN

SEAM ALLOWANCE INCLUDED IN CLOTHES PATTERN

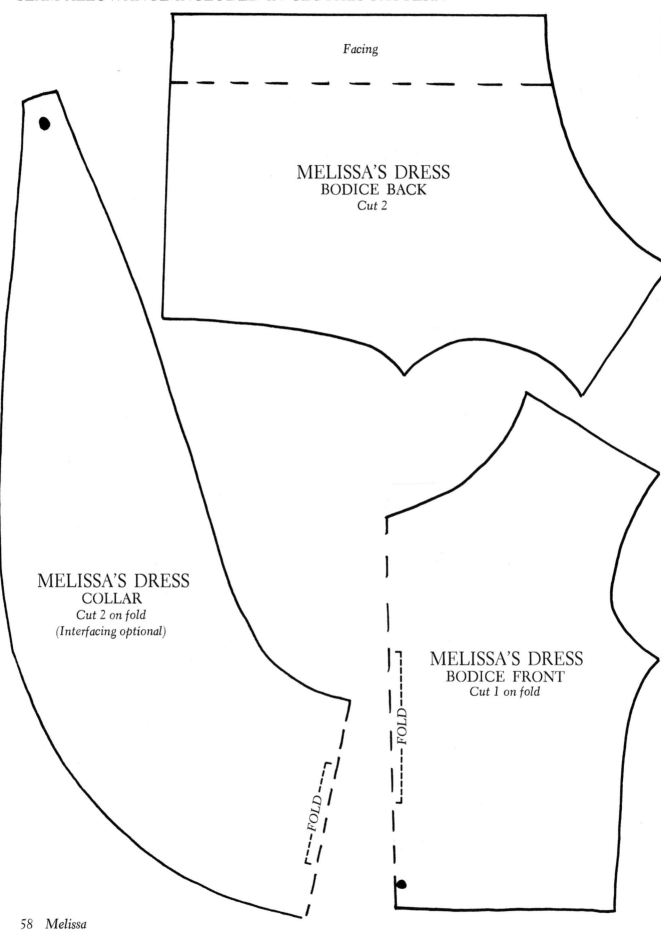

Facing

MELISSA'S DRESS
BODICE BACK
Cut 2

MELISSA'S DRESS
COLLAR
Cut 2 on fold
(Interfacing optional)

MELISSA'S DRESS
BODICE FRONT
Cut 1 on fold

FOLD

FOLD

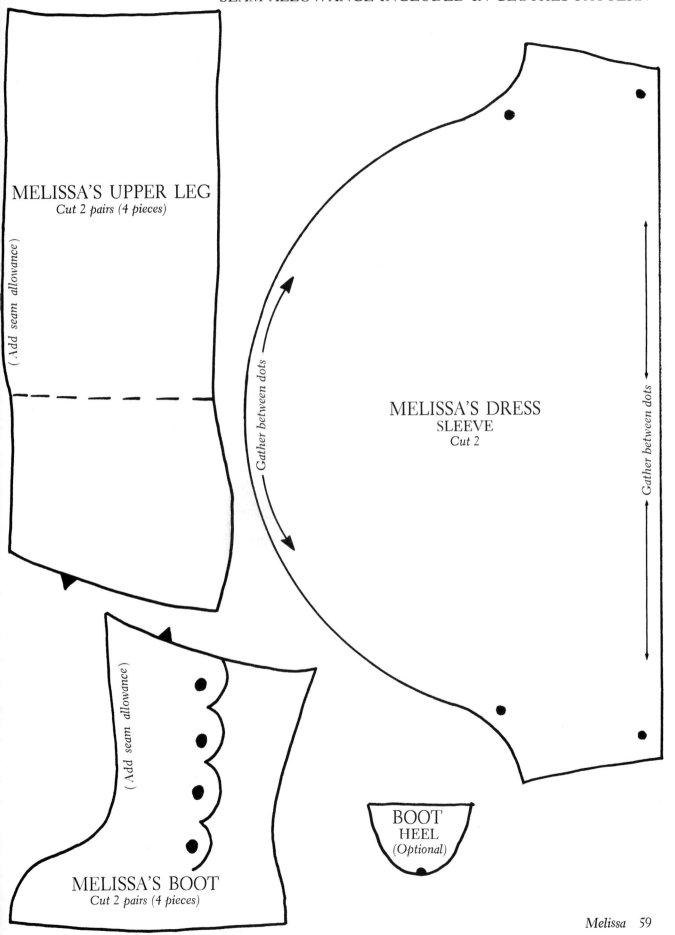

MELISSA'S UPPER LEG
Cut 2 pairs (4 pieces)

(Add seam allowance)

Gather between dots

MELISSA'S DRESS
SLEEVE
Cut 2

Gather between dots

(Add seam allowance)

MELISSA'S BOOT
Cut 2 pairs (4 pieces)

BOOT
HEEL
(Optional)

60 Belle

Belle, 1860's

Skirts reached huge proportions during this decade, and an uncomfortable metal hoop was worn beneath the skirt to accentuate the proportions. It was not unusual for 30 yards of fabric to be used to make a ball gown. Belle's headdress consists of colored lace formed into loops, a silver comb and a gold snood.

MATERIALS

FABRICS

BODY
⅓ yard skin color

DRESS
1 yard taffeta
1½ yards lightweight cotton lace
1½ yards silk organza
Note: All of these fabrics must be the same color.

SHOES
5″ × 10″ piece of satin
5″ × 10″ piece of interfacing

UNDERWEAR
For underwear materials, see pages 14-22.

NOTIONS AND TRIMMINGS

BODY
Embroidery threads: medium brown, blue, black, white and pink
2 ounces orange yarn *(for hair)*
6″ piece ¼″ ribbon to match hair
Gold or silver hairnet
Tiny pearl beads *(for necklace)*
2 yards ½″ colored lace *(optional for headdress)*
Silver comb *(optional)*

DRESS
7 yards ¼″ ribbon to match dress *(optional)*
Snaps
1 yard feather boning

BELLE'S FACE

Entire face is embroidered with three strands of embroidery thread. Begin with irises. Use close buttonhole stitch or satin stitch. Next, do pupils in satin stitch with black thread.

Eyes and eyebrows are outlined with medium brown in outline stitch.

Mouth is done in two sections with pink satin stitch.

If you wish, rouge cheeks and lightly shade inner eye and along nose with brown colored pencil.

BELLE'S HAIR

Following hairline on pattern and using two strands of yarn, cover head with large back stitches. Your stitches can be ¾″ or longer.

Cut a piece of cardboard 24″ × 6″. Wind yarn around cardboard enough times to have strands cover a piece of matching ribbon 6″ long, with strands slightly overlapping for fullness. Cut along one edge of yarn to remove cardboard.

Stitch center of strands along both edges of ribbon. Use matching thread, as this stitching will show. With ribbon facing doll's scalp, stitch ribbon securely to scalp. Add a few extra strands at center front, if necessary, to cover end of ribbon.

Drape hair loosely down below ears, following backstitched hair. Pull hair to back from this point, and tie in a knot at nape of neck. Tuck ends under, and with matching yarn, stitch around knot to keep in place. Cover knot with gold or silver hairnet for snood. You may decorate snood with tiny flowers, if you wish.

BELLE'S COSTUME

UNDERWEAR

Use pantalettes on page 16.

DRESS

BODICE
1. Cut one bodice of lace and two of taffeta. One taffeta bodice is used for lining and one for interlining.

2. Baste lace bodice pieces to one set of the taffeta bodice (interlining) and handle as one fabric.

3. Stitch darts in bodice front.

4. Stitch shoulder seams.

5. Cut sleeves of lace only. Leave sleeve folded as cut. Through both thicknesses of lace run gathering stitches along upper sleeve. Pull up to fit armhole and stitch to armhole.

6. Sew side seams.

7. The remaining taffeta bodice pieces are to be used as the lining. Sew darts in taffeta bodice front and sew shoulder and side seams.

8. Right sides together, sew lining to bodice, starting at back waist and continuing completely around to same point on the other side of the back waist. Clip lining if necessary; turn to inside and press neck and back edges.

SKIRT

1. Before cutting, make certain that organza, taffeta and lace are the same width.

2. Cut the following pieces:
Taffeta: one strip 14″ by the width of the fabric
Organza: 3 strips 9″ by width of the fabric
Lace: one strip 2½″ by the width of the fabric
    4 strips 5½″ by the width of the fabric

3. Seam together short ends of taffeta piece, leaving 2½″ open for back opening at top (waist). Press seam open.

4. Measure down 9″ from waist. Stitch feather boning on inside at this point, overlapping boning about 1″ at center back. It is easiest to use the zipper foot on your sewing machine for this. Stitch on both sides of boning.

5. Fold up and press a ¾″ hem in bottom. Do not hem stitch at this time. Set this piece aside.

6. Seam together short ends of one organza strip, leaving 2½″ open for back opening at waist.

7. Sew remaining organza strips together into a circle for bottom ruffle. Fold in half and press, making a strip that is 4½″.

8. Baste short lace strip to waistline of organza skirt.

9. Seam remaining four lace strips, two at a time, into two circles for remaining skirt ruffles. If desired, trim lace ruffles with ribbon.

10. Run gathering stitches around the three ruffles (2 lace; 1 organza) and pull up stitches to fit organza skirt.

11. Right sides together, stitch bottom ruffle to bottom of organza skirt. Press seam toward waistline.

12. Remaining two ruffles are sewn on so that stitches from previous rows cannot be seen. Stitch flat to organza skirt.

13. Slip taffeta hoop skirt inside organza skirt. Run two rows of gathering stitches through all thicknesses. Pull up as tightly as possible.

Note: If you prefer making the skirt with all lace ruffles, cut six strips of lace 5½″ by the width of the fabric and seam together the six lace strips into circles for skirt ruffles. Only one strip of organza, 9″ by the width of the fabric, will be necessary for the organza skirt.

JOINING THE DRESS

1. Baste bodice to skirt, being careful not to catch in bodice lining.

2. Stitch waistline seam twice for strength.

3. Turn under raw edges of bodice lining at waistline and handstitch in place. Tack lining armholes to armholes of bodice.

4. Close back with snaps.

5. Check length of taffeta underskirt and hem. The underskirt should not show below the ruffles.

SHOES

1. Cut uppers and sole of iron-on interfacing (no seam allowance) and press on satin before cutting satin with seam allowance.

2. If desired, embroider a tiny design on uppers.

3. Stitch center back seam on uppers.

4. Right sides together, stitch uppers to sole placing dot at center back. Turn.

5. If desired, glue cardboard innersoles to wrong side of satin and cut out (no seam allowance). Slip inside shoes.

FINISHING TOUCHES

1. Fold colored lace in half three times.

2. Gather in center and tack on head.

3. Put comb in back knot.

4. Put pearls around neck.

BELLE'S FACE

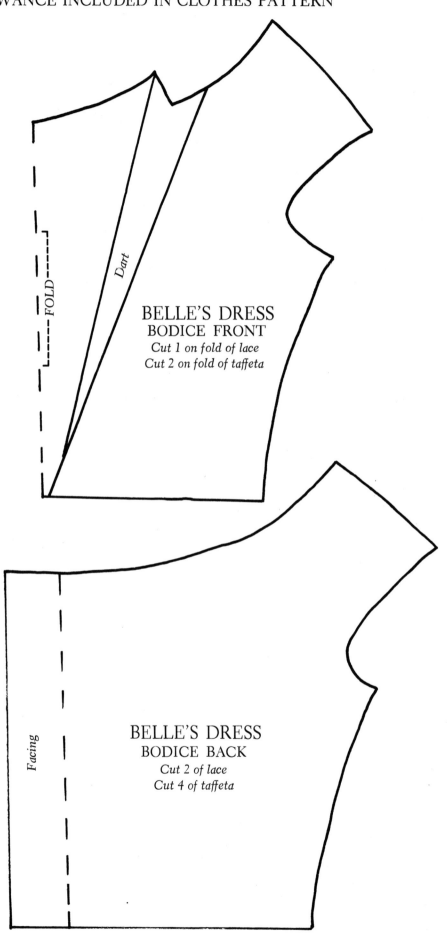

FOLD

Dart

BELLE'S DRESS
BODICE FRONT
Cut 1 on fold of lace
Cut 2 on fold of taffeta

Facing

BELLE'S DRESS
BODICE BACK
Cut 2 of lace
Cut 4 of taffeta

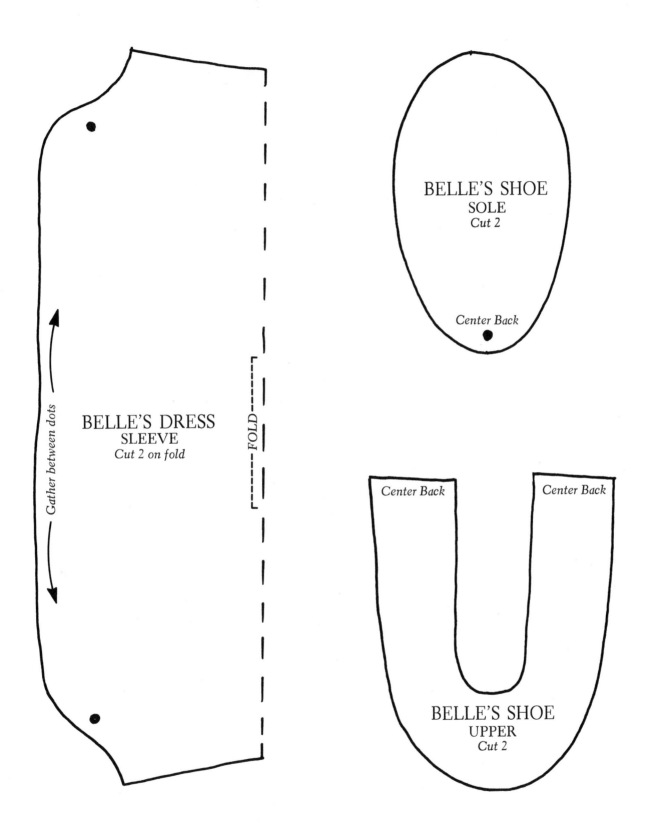

BELLE'S SHOE
SOLE
Cut 2

Center Back

Gather between dots

BELLE'S DRESS
SLEEVE
Cut 2 on fold

FOLD

Center Back   *Center Back*

BELLE'S SHOE
UPPER
Cut 2

66 *Jocelyn*

Jocelyn, 1870's

Jocelyn's face comes right from the pages of *Godey's Lady's Book*, the magazine for nineteenth-century women. Her dress is a very simplified version of the elaborately decorated dresses of the time. If you desire, you can decorate your doll with lace handkerchiefs, ribbons, flowers, ruffles—just about anything you wish. The bustle which Jocelyn wears was an important fashion feature of this period.

MATERIALS

FABRICS

BODY
1/3 yard skin color

DRESS
1½ yards striped taffeta

PETTICOAT
½ yard white batiste

BOOTS (OR SHOES)
5″ × 10″ piece of black cotton (*or felt*)

UNDERWEAR
For underwear materials, see pages 14-22.

NOTIONS AND TRIMMINGS

BODY
Embroidery threads: dark brown, light brown, black, white, dark green, light green, pink
1 ounce yarn (*for hair*)

DRESS
Beads or tiny buttons
½ yard 2½″ lace for trimming sleeves (*optional*)
Snaps

BOOTS
8 small black beads for "buttons" (*optional*)

OPTIONAL
Scrap of fake or real fur (*for muff*)
Feathers and flowers
earrings or 2 pearl-head pins

JOCELYN'S FACE

Jocelyn's face is admittedly very homely; however, if you have ever seen fashion sketches for this period, such as in *Godey's Lady's Book*, you will notice that almost every sketch has this type of face, with difficult, three-quarter pose and very prominent nose. If you cannot put this homely face on such a beautifully dressed doll, an alternate face has been provided. For alternate face, use three strands of embroidery floss for iris, pupil and mouth. Use two strands for outline of eyes and eyebrows, and two strands for nostrils.

For three-quarter face, use two strands of light brown embroidery floss to outline nose. Use three strands for rest of face. Rouge cheeks if desired, and lightly shade face along the length of the nose with brown colored pencil.

JOCELYN'S HAIR

Following hairline, backstitch hairline all the way around head, keeping a defined center part. Completely cover entire head with backstitches. Your stitches can be ¾″ or longer. Keep the rows of stitches close together, so that scalp does not show through.

With six strands of yarn about 24″ long, make a twisted cord; fold in half and twist again, so that you will have one thick "curl" about 4″ long. Tie ends with a matching strand of yarn, leaving an end for sewing. Sew to back of head at hairline, so that it will hang down doll's back.

With four strands of yarn about 14″ long, make another twisted cord. Arrange this cord into several small curls. Secure with matching yarn, then sew to top of doll's head, hiding ends under curls.

JOCELYN'S LEGS

Cut "boots" from black fabric, being sure to add seam allowances. Stay stitch upper curved edge, and carefully clip. Sew boot to upper leg matching notches. Complete legs as described on page 2. After stuffing, embroider "closing" on outsides using an outline stitch. Sew on beads for buttons.

Optional Methods (1) Use the regular leg pattern on page 9 and paint boots on with textile paint or waterproof markers. Use the boot portion of the leg pattern as a guide for painting. Add "buttons" as above, if desired.

(2) Make the regular legs according to pattern on page 9 and instructions on page 2. Follow the instructions on page 69 for shoes.

JOCEYLN'S COSTUME

UNDERWEAR

Use knee length pantalettes on page 16, corset on page 21, bust shaper and bustle shaper on page 22.

PETTICOAT

1. Cut a waistband the length of the doll's waist measure plus one inch.
2. Cut fabric 12″ long by the width of the fabric.
3. Run two rows of gathering stitches at waistline.
4. Gather petticoat to fit waistband, putting most of the gathers in the back. Depending upon the weight of fabric used, you will most likely have more gathered material than you have waistband. Do not be concerned; simply fold pleats in the gathered fabric, at the back of the petticoat on either side of the back opening. This will simply help the bustle shaper do the work of emphasizing the bustle look at the back of the dress.

TWO-PIECE DRESS

JACKET

1. Sew darts in jacket back and jacket front. Join at shoulder seams.
2. Sew front and back facings together at notches.
3. To make ruffle: cut a strip of dress fabric 1½″ × 18″. Press in half lengthwise. At each end of folded strip, cut away a triangular piece starting ¼″ from folded edge, cutting to nothing at raw edge.

Folded Edge

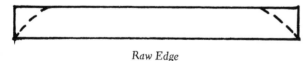

Raw Edge

Run two rows of gathering stitches along raw edge. Pull up to fit right front, around back neck to the edge of left front opening. (*Point of "V"*)

4. Pin ruffle *and* jacket facing to jacket and stitch in place.
5. Face sleeve with sleeve facing. Ease sleeve into armhole and stitch.
6. Stitch sleeve and side seams of jacket in one continuous stitching.

7. Line peplum pieces, leaving waist edges open for turning. Turn.

8. Starting at center back and with right sides together, pin peplum pieces to jacket. Fold front facings to outside over peplum. Stitch entire lower edge of jacket. Turn facings back to inside. Press seam towards jacket. Make buttonholes on right front and sew on buttons.

9. If desired, the sleeves may be trimmed with a lace ruffle that will fall over the hand. With elastic thread, gather lace to fit wrist of doll about ½″ to ¾″ from finished edge of lace. Make seam in raw end of the lace and gather upper edge of lace to fit inside sleeve. Tack lace over facings on wrong side of sleeve.

10. To make dress bustle: cut a piece of dress fabric 4½″ by the width of the fabric. Fold in half, right sides together, and stitch along long ends. Do not press. Turn to right side. Stitch short ends together. Using the short, stitched ends as tacking point, arrange bustle in loops and tack in place. Then tack bustle to peplum of jacket at center back as in illustration.

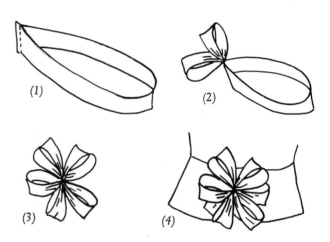

SKIRT

1. Cut two skirts, each 14″ by the width of the fabric.
2. Turn up each skirt 1″ and hem.
3. On upper skirt, locate center front, and run two rows of gathering stitches from hem to about halfway up the front. Pull up gathers as tight as possible. If desired, apply a self ruffle to the under skirt at hem edge. Cover raw edge with matching velvet ribbon.
4. Cut a waistband the length of the doll's waist plus 1¼″.
5. Treating both skirts as one fabric, run gathering stitches through the skirts at waistline.
6. As with petticoat, pull up gathers to fit the waistband, putting most of the gathers in the back. You will need to fold pleats into the gathered material at the back.
7. Finish with snaps or hooks and eyes.

SHOES
(or follow instructions for making boots on page 67)

1. Right sides together join shoe uppers at center back.
2. Rights sides together stitch upper to sole, placing dot at center back.
3. Trim close stitching and turn.
4. If you wish, embroider a design on upper.

FINISHING TOUCHES

1. Make muff by folding a scrap of fur around doll's hands.
2. Add feathers and/or flowers to doll's hair.

Note: If doll is to be washable, don't attach finishing touches permanently. Simply pin them in a pleasing arrangement so that they can be removed when the doll is washed.

JOCELYN'S FACE

ALLOW FOR SEAMS WHEN CUTTING HEAD

ALTERNATE FACE FOR JOCELYN

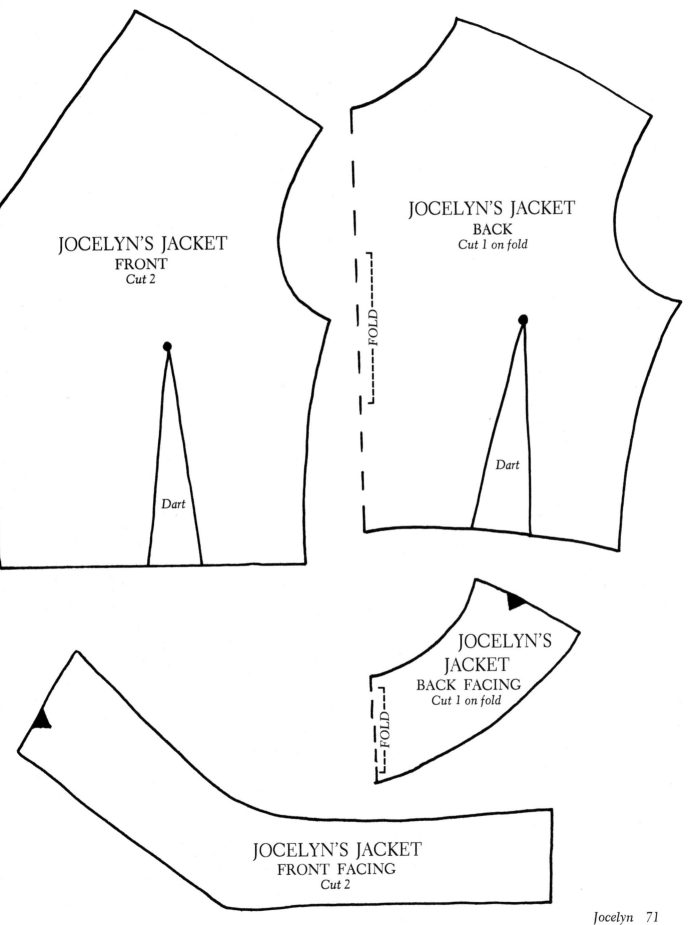

JOCELYN'S JACKET
FRONT
Cut 2

Dart

JOCELYN'S JACKET
BACK
Cut 1 on fold

FOLD

Dart

JOCELYN'S
JACKET
BACK FACING
Cut 1 on fold

FOLD

JOCELYN'S JACKET
FRONT FACING
Cut 2

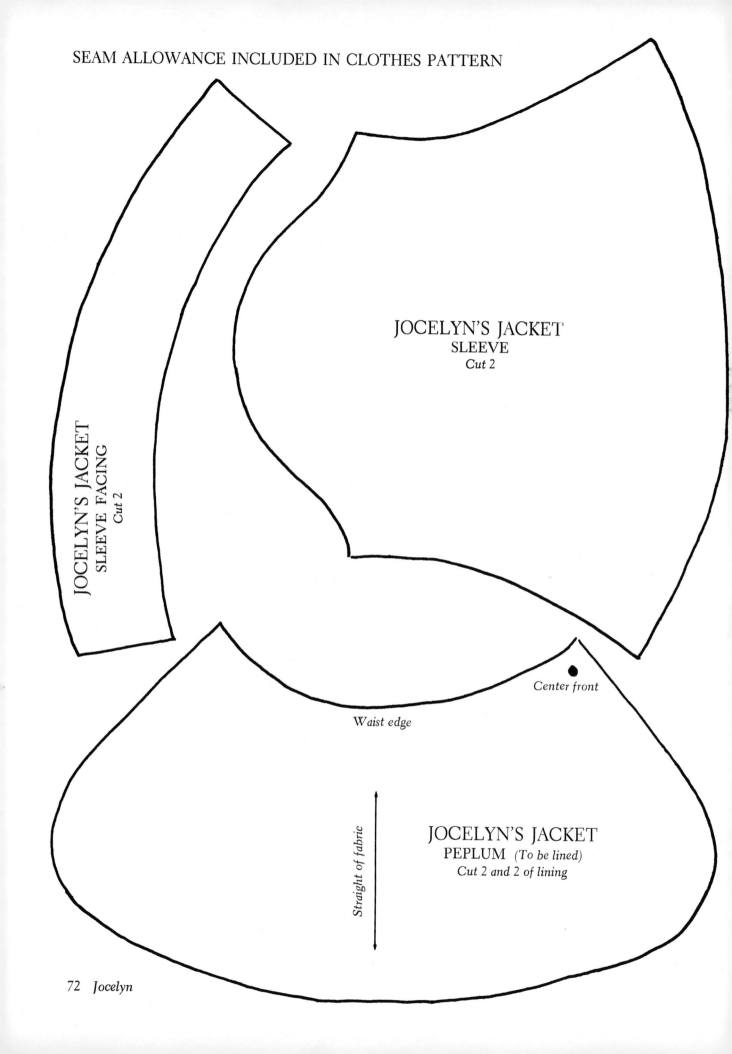

SEAM ALLOWANCE INCLUDED IN CLOTHES PATTERN

JOCELYN'S JACKET
SLEEVE
Cut 2

JOCELYN'S JACKET
SLEEVE FACING
Cut 2

Center front

Waist edge

Straight of fabric

JOCELYN'S JACKET
PEPLUM *(To be lined)*
Cut 2 and 2 of lining

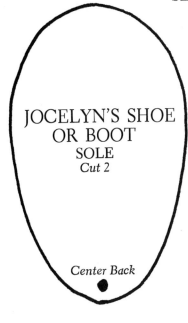

JOCELYN'S SHOE
OR BOOT
SOLE
Cut 2

Center Back

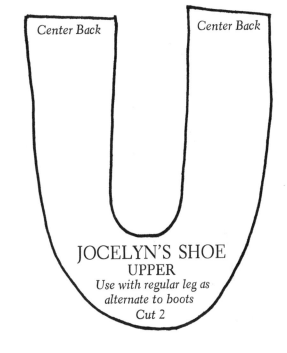

Center Back   Center Back

JOCELYN'S SHOE
UPPER
*Use with regular leg as
alternate to boots*
Cut 2

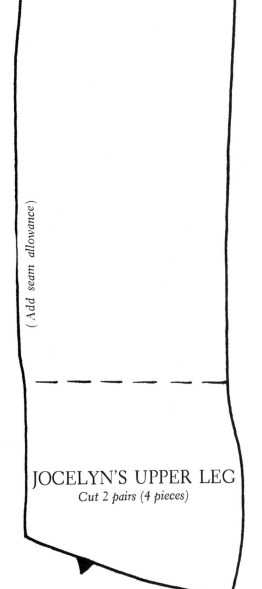

(Add seam allowance)

JOCELYN'S UPPER LEG
Cut 2 pairs (4 pieces)

(Add seam allowance)

JOCELYN'S BOOT
Cut 2 pairs (4 pieces)

74 *Penelope*

Penelope, 1890's

In the 1890's a form called the "hourglass" figure became the dominant silhouette. Ballooning sleeves and widening skirts helped to make the tightly corseted waist seem even smaller, giving the figure the appearance of two separate round masses joined in the middle. The neck was almost always covered, either by the collar of the dress, or by a wide choker of velvet when a low-necked ball gown was worn.

MATERIALS

FABRICS

BODY
⅓ yard skin color

DRESS
1 yard taffeta

PETTICOAT
½ yard white batiste

SHOES
5″ × 10″ square of felt (*to match dress*)

UNDERWEAR
For underwear materials, see pages 14-22.

NOTIONS AND TRIMMINGS

BODY
Embroidery threads: sage green, pink, white, black, light brown
1 ounce yarn (*for hair*)

DRESS
1 yard 3″ wide flat, heavy lace trim
Snaps

PETTICOAT
1½ yards ½″ lace ruffling (*optional*)

OPTIONAL
Earrings and 2 pearl-head straight pins

PENELOPE'S FACE

Use one strand of light brown embroidery thread for eyebrows. The rest of the face is done with three strands. Eyelashes, nostrils and the outline of the eye are brown. Irises are sage green; pupils black; mouth pink.

It is best to do the irises first; then the pupils; then outline the eye and do lashes. If desired, highlight eyes with white after eyes are completely embroidered. Rouge cheeks with pink colored pencil.

PENELOPE'S HAIR

Following hairline, cover head with large back stitches. Hair should look as though it were all pulled to the top of the head. To make topknot, twist four 30″ strands of yarn into a twisted cord. Form cord into several short "curls" and tack securely to the top of the head.

PENELOPE'S COSTUME

UNDERWEAR

Use knee length pantalettes on page 16, corset on page 21, bust shaper and bustle shaper on page 22.

PETTICOAT

1. Cut fabric 14″ long by the width of the fabric.
2. Cut a waistband the length of the doll's waist measurement plus one inch.
3. Run two rows of gathering stitches at waistline.
4. Pull up gathers to fit waistband, having most of the gathers across the back, with just a slight gathering across the front. If you have more gathered material than will fit in the waistband, simply fold pleats in the gathered material at the back. This will help the bustle shaper do its job of holding out the back of the dress.
5. Attach snaps or buttons at back closing.
6. Hem the petticoat, making certain that it does not show beneath the dress.

DRESS

1. Sew darts in bodice back and bodice front.
2. Stitch the wide, flat lace trim to center of bodice

front. Cut away lace at top following the curve of the neckline.

3. Sew shoulder seams.

4. Fold collar in half lengthwise and stitch ends. Turn right side out and press.

5. Cut section from the heavy lace trim and sew to collar. This will hold the collar firmly as well as add a decorative touch.

6. Stay stitch neck of dress, clipping where necessary. Sew collar to dress.

7. Run gathering stitches in sleeve at armhole and lower edge of upper sleeve.

8. Pull up gathers to fit lower sleeve and stitch lower sleeve to upper sleeve.

9. Stitch sleeve facing to lower edge of lower sleeve.

10. Pull up gathers at armhole edge to fit armhole and stitch in place.

11. Sew sleeve, facing and side seam of bodice in one continuous stitching. Fold in facings and stitch in place.

12. Cut a section from the lace trim and trim sleeves, allowing the lace edge to fall over the hand.

13. Cut skirt 14″ by the width of the fabric. Press up one inch at lower edge and hem.

14. Locate the center front of the skirt and stitch the lace trim up the center front.

15. Run gathering stitches at waist edge of skirt. Pull up to fit bodice. If you have gathered extra material, simply fold a pleat in the gathered fabric at the back. Stitch to top.

16. Sew center back skirt to within three inches of waistline with a ⅝″ seam.

17. Sew snaps to back for closing.

18. To make bustle; cut a piece of dress fabric 5″ by the width of the fabric. Seam the long end. Turn right side out. Sew into a ring and arrange the ring in several attractive loops, tacking where necessary to hold. Attach at back waistline.

SHOES

1. Right sides together join the shoe uppers at center back.

2. Right sides together stitch upper to sole, placing dot at center back.

3. Trim close to stitching and turn.

4. If you wish, embroider a design on the upper.

FINISHING TOUCHES

(*Optional*) Remove drops from earrings. Put pearl-headed straight pin through drop and attach to doll.

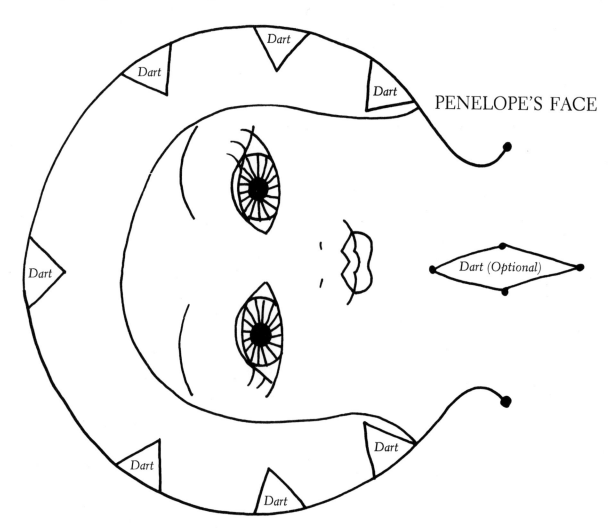

PENELOPE'S FACE

ALLOW FOR SEAMS WHEN CUTTING HEAD

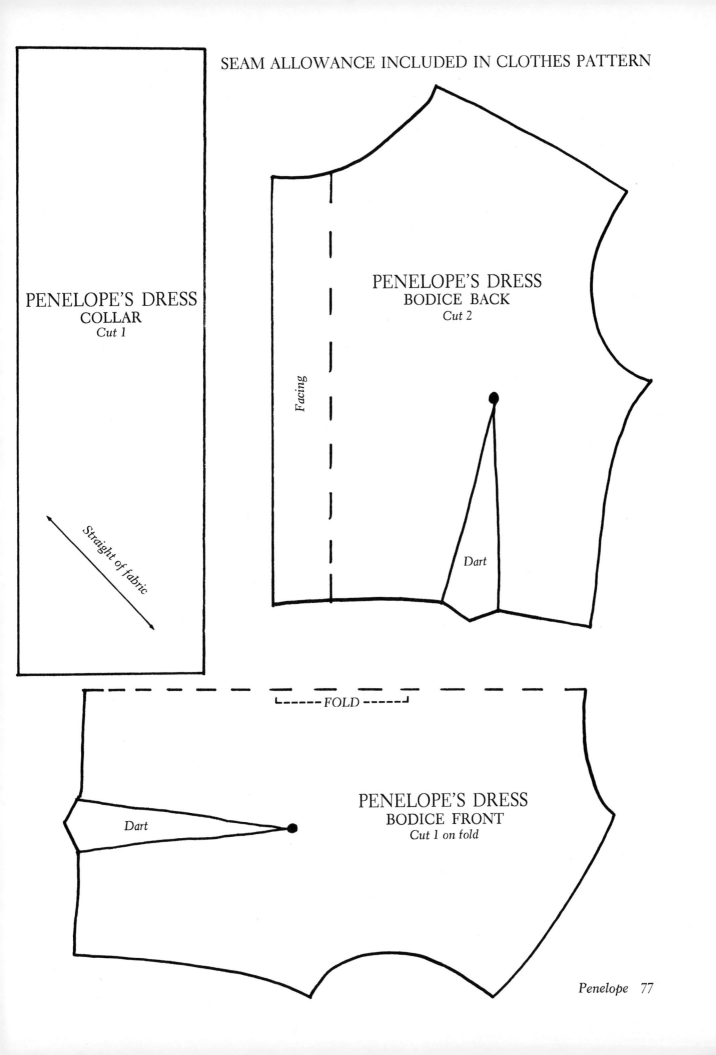

SEAM ALLOWANCE INCLUDED IN CLOTHES PATTERN

PENELOPE'S DRESS
COLLAR
Cut 1

Straight of fabric

PENELOPE'S DRESS
BODICE BACK
Cut 2

Facing

Dart

FOLD

Dart

PENELOPE'S DRESS
BODICE FRONT
Cut 1 on fold

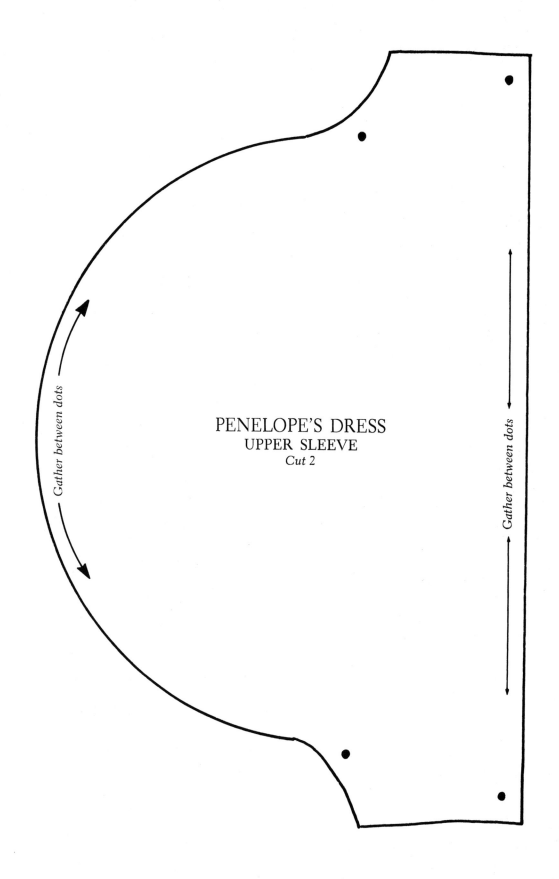

PENELOPE'S DRESS
UPPER SLEEVE
Cut 2

Gather between dots

Gather between dots

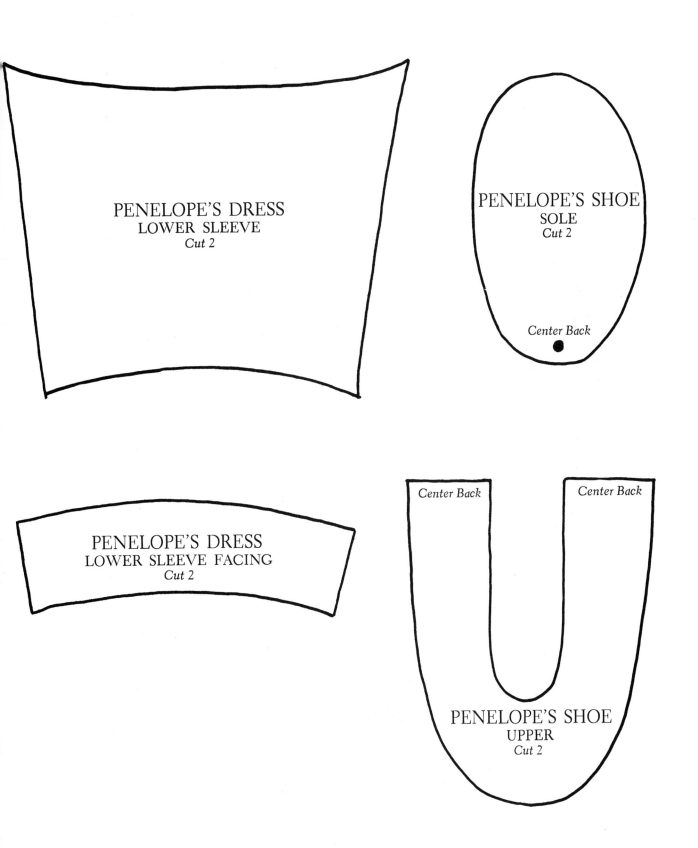

PENELOPE'S DRESS
LOWER SLEEVE
Cut 2

PENELOPE'S SHOE
SOLE
Cut 2

Center Back

PENELOPE'S DRESS
LOWER SLEEVE FACING
Cut 2

Center Back

Center Back

PENELOPE'S SHOE
UPPER
Cut 2

80   *Seminole Lady*

Seminole Lady

The Seminole Indians are to this day famous for their intricate patchwork. The women's skirts and the men's shirts consist of colorful fabric sewn into long strips, cut into various shapes, then resewn into new strips to create beautiful designs. Lace and rickrack are also added to further enhance the design. Yards of beads complete the authentic Seminole costume.

MATERIALS

FABRICS

BODY
⅓ yard pale rust fabric

DRESS
½ yard turquoise cotton
⅛ yard white cotton
⅛ yard purple cotton
⅛ yard red cotton
⅛ yard yellow cotton
¼ yard yellow batiste

NOTIONS AND TRIMMINGS

BODY
Embroidery threads: black, white, brown, pink
2 ounces black yarn (for hair)
¼" black ribbon (to match yarn)

DRESS
Red baby rickrack
Green baby rickrack
White rickrack
Red rickrack
¾ yard white lace edging
Snaps
Hook and eye

OPTIONAL
Strands of tiny beads

SEMINOLE LADY'S FACE

With one strand of black embroidery thread, take single, tiny stitches for eyebrows. This will give a natural brow line. The eyes are outlined with two strands of black embroidery thread, and the rest of the face is embroidered with three strands. The irises are brown; pupils black; nostrils black and mouth pink. Do the irises first; then pupils; then outline the eyes and do the lashes. After the eyes are completely embroidered, do the whites of the eyes on this doll to make her eyes really show up. Rouge cheeks, and shade at inner eyes and along nose with colored pencils.

SEMINOLE LADY'S HAIR

Starting at lower front head, cover head with large back stitches. Leave several long strands at each side of the front of the head.

Cut a piece of ¼" wide black ribbon the measurement of doll's head from ear to ear, plus ¼"

Cut a piece of cardboard 20" long by the width of the measurement of the doll's head from ear to ear plus ¼". Wrap cardboard loosely with yarn. Cut along one edge. (There should be enough yarn to cover the ribbon, with strands slightly overlapped for fullness.) Stitch center of yarn strands to ribbon. Stitch on both sides of the ribbon for strength.

With half of the yarn hanging in doll's face, stitch ribbon along hairline, stitching around front head and both sides of the ribbon. Pull hair to the back of the head. Trim straight around the head making certain that hair is even and approximately 2" below the shoulders.

SEMINOLE LADY'S COSTUME

UNDERWEAR

Doll wears no underwear.

OVERSKIRT

Following the color scheme provided in the diagram

on page 85, cut strips of colored cotton to widths indicated on the color scheme. *These measurements include ¼" seams.* All of the strips are 18" long.

Trim the strips as indicated and sew together to make overskirt.

To make patchwork strips:

1. Red and turquoise strip: Cut two strips each of red and turquoise to measure 1¼" × 18". Seam a red strip to a turquoise strip lengthwise, making two strips of red and turquoise. Cut one strip into bias patches. Cut the other strip into bias patches, reversing the direction; keep the piles separate.

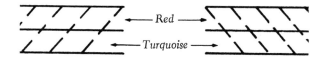

Now seam a patch from one pile to a patch from the other pile to get a design like this:

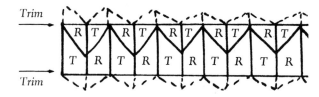

Trim the edges straight. You will need a strip 18" long.

2. Purple and red strip: Seam together lengthwise a 1" purple strip and a ¾" red strip. Cut into 1½" lengths and stitch back together vertically. You will need a strip 18" long.

DRESS

1. Cut bodice pieces from turquoise fabric.
2. Join shoulder seams of bodice front and back.
3. Press in facings and finish neck edge with self bias strip.
4. Sew one edge of a self bias strip to armholes.

5. Sew side seams.
6. Turn in bias strips at armholes and hem in place.
7. Cut turquoise fabric for skirt 9⅛" × 18".
8. Run gathering stitches in skirt and overskirt. Pull up to fit bodice with facings opened out. Stitch skirt and overskirt to bodice.
9. Seam skirt back in ⅝" seam to within 2" of waistline. Seam overskirt back in ⅝" seam to within 2" of waistline. Press seams open and hem facings separately to inside.
10. Hem skirts and close back with snaps.

CAPE

1. Cut a 1" wide bias strip of yellow batiste equal to the circumference of the doll's neck plus 1".
2. Cut a strip of turquoise cotton 3" × 18". Cut a strip of yellow batiste 2½" × 18". Seam the strips together lengthwise, and press seam toward the yellow batiste. Fold the yellow batiste in half on inside and hem over seam.
3. Stitch white lace edging along the edge of the yellow batiste. Cover the stitching with green baby rickrack. Stitch regular red rickrack on the yellow batiste next to the green rickrack. Stitch another row of green baby rickrack over the hem at the top of the yellow batiste.
4. Seam at center back from lower edge to just past yellow batiste strip.
5. Run gathering stitches at neck edge and pull up to fit bias strip. Stitch bias strip to cape and hem to inside. Close with hook and eye.

SHOES

Doll wears no shoes.

FINISHING TOUCHES

Seminole ladies love beads and wear strings and strings of them. Use tiny beads and as many strands as you want.

SEMINOLE LADY'S FACE

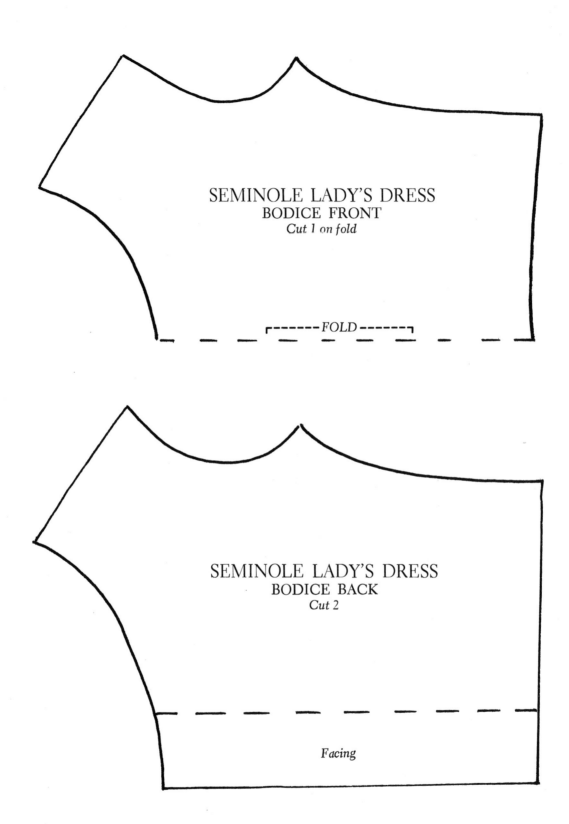

SEMINOLE LADY'S DRESS
BODICE FRONT
Cut 1 on fold

┌------FOLD------┐

SEMINOLE LADY'S DRESS
BODICE BACK
Cut 2

Facing

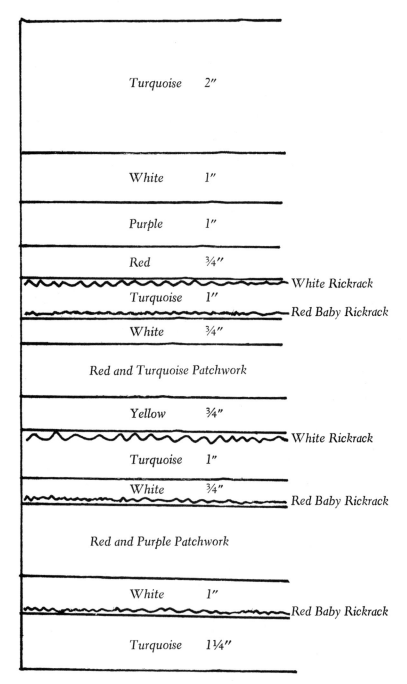

Turquoise   2″

White   1″

Purple   1″

Red   ¾″

White Rickrack

Turquoise   1″

Red Baby Rickrack

White   ¾″

Red and Turquoise Patchwork

Yellow   ¾″

White Rickrack

Turquoise   1″

White   ¾″

Red Baby Rickrack

Red and Purple Patchwork

White   1″

Red Baby Rickrack

Turquoise   1¼″

SEMINOLE LADY'S OVERSKIRT
DIAGRAM

86 *Hiruko*

Hiruko, a Lady of Japan

The ceremonial kimono of Japan, traditionally made of sumptuous fabrics with a minimum of cutting, is sewn together by hand. When it is cleaned, it is carefully taken apart, the pieces cleaned separately and then sewn back together. Needless to say, this is a very expensive and time consuming process so the lovely kimonos are worn only on very special occasions. For the sake of authenticity, you may wish to sew your kimono by hand. If so, use a very small running stitch and do not clip the fabric.

MATERIALS

FABRICS

BODY
⅓ yard off-white (*do not use yellow*)

SLIP
½ yard china silk, handkerchief linen or lightweight cotton

KIMONO
½ yard silk brocade or lightweight embroidered fabric

SLIPPERS
5″ × 10″ piece white cotton knit

NOTIONS AND TRIMMINGS

BODY
Embroidery threads: Black, dark brown, white, peachy pink
2 ounces black yarn (*for hair*)
½ yard ¼″ black ribbon

SLIP
⅜″ × 9″ piece of plastic (*for stiffening*)

KIMONO
2 hooks and eyes
1¼ yards 1½″ embroidered ribbon (*for obi*)
1 yard very narrow ribbon
2½ yards 1½″ satin binding to match Kimono

OPTIONAL
Flowers, baubles (*for hair*)

HIRUKO'S FACE

Use three strands of embroidery thread throughout, but make eyebrows thicker, where indicated, with additional rows of outline stitch. Irises are brown; pupils and nose black; mouth, peachy pink. It is best to do irises first, using a close buttonhole stitch or a satin stitch. Next do pupils with satin stitch. Outline eyes with black, filling in upper lid with additional rows of outline stitch. Mouth is satin stitch; nose is satin stitch or French knots. Cheeks can be rouged with pink colored pencil.

HIRUKO'S HAIR

Following hairline and using two strands of yarn in the needle, cover the head with large backstitches. All stitches should go from the front hairline to the back to give the effect of the hair being pulled back from the face.

Side view of Hiruko's hair

Cut a piece of ½" wide black ribbon the measurement of the doll's head from ear to ear plus ¼". Cut a piece of cardboard 20" long by the measurement of the doll's head plus ¼". Wrap cardboard loosely with yarn. Cut along one edge. (*There should be enough yarn to cover the ribbon, with strands slightly overlapping for fullness.*) Stitch center of yarn strands to ribbon. Stitch on both sides of the ribbon for strength.

With the hair hanging in the doll's face, sew the ribbon to the front hairline. Don't try to curve around the "widow's peak" at center front; sew just above it.

Pull all of the hair to the crown, and with a matching strand of yarn, tie a ponytail about one inch from the scalp. Tie again about 2¾" from first tie, and again about 1½" from the ends of the hair. Secure the bun by sewing with matching yarn all around, tucking in ends so that they won't show. (*See illustration.*)

Decorate hairdo with flowers, baubles, etc.

HIRUKO'S COSTUME

KIMONO

Cutting and Shaping

1. For back, cut a piece of brocade 8" × 17". Fold piece in half lengthwise, place guide at folded edge and cut neckline.

2. For front, cut two pieces 6" × 17". Using cutting guide for front, line up guide with side edge at top. Cut front necklines as indicated, tapering cutting line gradually out to edge.

3. For sleeves, cut two pieces 5" × 22".

Sewing

1. Sew shoulder seams.

2. Right sides together, stitch satin binding all around one edge. Press seam allowances toward binding. Press ¼" to wrong side on other long side of binding. Press binding in half to wrong side and slip stitch to wrong side to finish.

3. Fold each sleeve piece in half to measure 5" × 11". Measure down 3" from folded edge and place a pin, front and back. This portion is the armhole. Place a pin at the shoulder. Match shoulder pin to shoulder seam, right sides together. Stitch between armhole pins.

4. Turn sleeve over body of garment so that right sides of sleeve are together. Stitch sleeve together from underarm to lower edge, across lower edge, then up to opposite side to point of underarm stitching. Press seams towards sleeve. Hem at wrist edge to finish sleeve.

5. Press up 1" along lower edge for hem. Blind hem in place.

OBI

(*Note: A real obi is a long sash tied to resemble a butterfly—a very difficult process. While the doll's obi is not authentic, it will look very much like a real obi when completed.*)

1. Cut a piece of the embroidered ribbon the width of the doll's waist plus ¾". Line with satin binding, and close with hooks and eyes.

2. Cut two pieces of embroidered ribbon 10¾" long. Leaving ends raw, line with satin. Join raw ends of each piece to form two circles.

3. Cut a 3" piece of embroidered ribbon and stitch ends together to form a circle.

4. Pull two large circles halfway through the small circle to form a double bow.

5. Tack bow over hooks and eyes on sash, and arrange bow to resemble a butterfly.

SLIP

(*Note: Slip is made the same as kimono, with the following exceptions.*)

1. Follow steps 1 through 4 for making kimono. Use a self binding, and do not slip stitch binding to wrong side.

2. Mark center back neckline of slip with a pin. Measure 4½" from pin around neckline on either side of pin. Slip stitch this portion in place to wrong side. Insert plastic stiffening for neckline. Now complete slip stitching to wrong side down both sides of front.

3. Hem slip so that it does not show beneath the kimono.

DRESSING DOLL

(*Note: There are no fasteners on Hiruko's garment.*)

1. Stuff sleeves of slip inside sleeves of kimono. Put both garments on doll.

2. Fold *left* front over *right* front of slip and tie at waist with narrow ribbon or string.

3. Fold *left* front over *right* front of kimono and tie in place the same way.

4. Hook obi at center back.

5. Arrange collar so that collar of slip shows above collar of kimono. Drape the collar at center back so that it has a graceful line and all of neck shows. The neck is considered one of the most beautiful parts of the Japanese woman.

SLIPPERS (*Optional*)

1. Join two pieces together by sewing along two short sides and one long side.

2. Narrowly hem open long side.

3. Repeat for other slipper.

4. Authentic slippers have a separate toe for the large toe and are worn outside under thong sandals, called zoris. If you wish, you can stitch the slippers to the foot, and create the illusion of a toe by stitching through the foot as you did for doll's fingers to form a big toe.

Dart

Dart

Dart

Dart

Dart

Dart

Dart

Dart

HIRUKO'S SLIPPERS
Cut 4

Dart (Optional)

HIRUKO'S FACE

HIRUKO'S KIMONO AND SLIP
BACK NECKLINE
Cutting Guide

HIRUKO'S KIMONO AND SLIP
FRONT NECKLINE
Cutting Guide

FOLD

SEAM ALLOWANCE INCLUDED IN CLOTHES PATTERN